BALANCING THE REQUEST TO BE GOOD

AN ASPECT OF THE ROOM

Balancing the Request to be Good

An Account of a Visit to the Outskirts of Child Psychotherapy

Sheila K. Cameron

FREE ASSOCIATION BOOKS/LONDON/NEW YORK

Published in 1995 by
Free Association Books Ltd
Omnibus Business Centre
39–41 North Road
London N7 9DP
and 70 Washington Square South
New York, NY 10012–1091

99   98   97   96   95
5   4   3   2   1

ISBN 1 85343 323 hardback

A CIP catalogue record for this book is available
from the British Library.

Produced for Free Association Books Ltd by
Chase Production Services, Chipping Norton
Typeset by Stanford DTP Services
Printed in the EC by The Cromwell Press,
Broughton Gifford, England

FOR AIMEE, LUCIE AND JOAN

It is symbolic thought which overcomes
the natural inertia of man and endows him
with a new ability, the ability constantly
to reshape his human universe.

Ernst Cassirer, *An Essay on Man.*

Contents

vii

List of Drawings

List of Photographs

Part I
Setting Out

1

ON THE WRONG ROAD

In the early 1970s I began working in a child guidance day-unit for children of primary school age who had been identified as having emotional and behavioural difficulties. Originally trained as a teacher of physical education, I had acquired extensive practical experience of working creatively with children of all ages in a variety of subjects and settings by the time I took up this particular position.

The first seven of my fourteen-year stay in the unit could in some respects be viewed as an apprenticeship. The person in charge during that time was someone from whom I learned a great deal. Had she remained there, the journey I am about to describe might well have followed a different route, but it would certainly have been an easier one.

What began to trouble me most about the work were those children who very obviously did not get any better. They just got bigger and were moved on. At various intervals after their departure, one heard tales of their running away, running wild, being moved from one institution to another and getting more distressed and deeper into trouble.

Apart from the ineffectiveness of my work, a further incitement to rethink what I was doing had come from some remarks made by a local and internationally respected child psychiatrist. He had stated publicly and quite unequivocally that unless child guidance units, such as the one in which I worked, had a formal therapeutic component as part of their provision, they were incapable of responding adequately to the needs of the majority of children referred to them. I only gradually came to understand what he meant.

It was against this background I became firmly convinced that I would need to find a more satisfactory way of working with the children if I were to remain at the unit. What follows is an account of some of the events which surrounded that attempt.

2

THE MIRACULOUS LEAFLET

At the height of my dissatisfaction with the work, I began some haphazard reading of Sigmund Freud. This reading had been encouraged by an eccentric local writer who, during a chance meeting one cold Sunday morning, had launched into enthusiastic praise of the literary merits of *The Psychopathology of Everyday Life* (Freud, [1901] 1960).

Before beginning to read his own words, I had read several biographies of Freud and had become genuinely interested in the lives and work of the men and women with whom he was associated during his life. An interest in those who came later, came later. A preference for reading what might be termed adult theorists is one which I have retained. At the time it produced a rather sparse overall knowledge of psychoanalytic psychotherapy in general and a pronounced ignorance about therapeutic work with children.

I had read books such as *The Piggle* (Winnicott, 1977) and *Dibs: In Search of Self* (Axline, 1964) and had gained, somewhere along the way, enough understanding of non-directive play therapy for it to be a useful influence during the early stages of this enquiry.

About the same time that my reading was getting serious, I decided to go into analysis for what I described to myself and others as personal and professional reasons. At the time I actually had no idea what this would entail, but it proved to be a very formative experience, not so much in relation to resolving my own problems, but in the way it increased my understanding of how I might help the children with theirs.

Coinciding with these circumstances came an opportunity to attend a year's course in Special Educational Needs at a local college of education. As I look back now, the course, the reading and the analysis were just several of the many life experiences, both old and new, which were about to be gathered in and used to develop an approach for which I could feel a genuine enthusiasm.

The course itself was almost entirely educational in its focus and the few references to therapy were usually attached to the word 'behavioural'. There was a marvellous library in the college and this was more than adequate compensation for other disappointments. Also, if it was attempted somewhat surreptitiously, there was just

4

enough space and opportunity for exploring one's own interests. The most potentially engaging requirement of the course was to write a dissertation on a subject of one's own choosing, albeit one which had a relevance to children with special needs.

With the uncertainty of someone reaching for a light switch in total darkness but knowing approximately where it is and anticipating illumination, my prevailing feeling at the time was that I had something important to do. Exactly what it was would only become apparent in its own good time. This is obviously not an attitude which can be easily accommodated in most institutes of learning. And so it proved.

The remarkably naive idea, which began to take precedence over all others, was to contrive and research a first interview situation. I would be sitting at a table across from a child, with various materials between us, and in the ensuing interaction their main concerns would be revealed. It is difficult now to believe I could have been so totally unaware of what educational psychologists do with children.

What I did know was that years before I had made a Christmas present for two young children by filling a solid wooden box with objects such as string, plasticine, scissors, paper, a stapler and pencils. I had then declared the box to be magic in that, if everything which was taken out of it was always returned, it would always be there when it was needed. It was a box similar to this but invested with an entirely different kind of magic that I had in mind.

In discussion with a senior member of staff it was felt that my ideas were not only too vague but, more importantly, they might lead me to trespass into areas of expertise generally accepted as the domain of other professional groups. I was asked to think again.

Some days later, perplexed about what my next move should be, I wandered aimlessly away from the psychology shelves to an area of the library I had not visited before. There I came across the section on art. I reached up to take down a book on developmental art and, as I did so, what I thought was a leaflet fell out of it onto the floor, at my feet. I picked it up and there on the first page was a detailed description of the sand tray and the small toys and objects which constitute the 'World Material' as devised by Margaret Lowenfeld. On the back page was the address of the writer, Ruth Pickford, who just happened to live several miles away from the college. A few hours later I had written her a letter. For several years after this she, and until his death her husband Professor Ralph Pickford, took a helpful interest in how the work progressed.

In a second discussion with the same lecturer, a reformulated proposal based on this new information was given official approval. Because of the way in which I had discovered the paper and because it provided me with an acceptable and fascinating subject for the dissertation, I chose for a long time to refer to it, with close friends only, as the miraculous leaflet. Later, when I began to encounter a host of difficulties, which I now understand to be an integral feature of most innovative endeavours, the circumstances in which I had found it probably inclined me away from dropping the whole lot over the nearest cliff.

3

AVOIDING MARGARET LOWENFELD

For reasons which I did not think about clearly at the time, it never occurred to me to study the ideas and theories on which Margaret Lowenfeld's particular kind of child psychotherapy were based. A major factor was undoubtedly the feeling that they reflected a very individual perception and experience, one which I found difficulty in relating to directly and which I feared might impinge on any hopes I had of making my own sense of the children's use of the materials.

Once I had found the list of toys, I immediately set about collecting them and, when they were unavailable in shops, arranging to have them made. Later I was preoccupied with the task of acquiring a suitably-sized sand tray and with the practical difficulties involved in taking clear photographs of the children's tray constructions.

Most of the information I did acquire about Margaret Lowenfeld's approach came from the book *The Lowenfeld World Technique* (Bowyer,[1] 1970) and from some of the papers to which it referred. I read only what I needed for the dissertation. This was rather a slight affair entitled 'Aspects of the Development and Use of Small Toys in Making Therapeutic Contact with Young Children'. Theoretically it touched on the pioneering work of Hermine von Hug-Hellmuth, Anna Freud and Melanie Klein, made passing reference to the importance of Jean Piaget and included superficial comment on the work of Margaret Lowenfeld. On the practical side it drew mainly on the observation of eight hours of play therapy and from the experience of introducing the sand-tray materials to over fifty children in a variety of educational settings.

My avoidance of Lowenfeld's ideas, although quite assiduous, was certainly not total. I particularly valued a description by Professor Pickford of his use of the World Material, for psychotherapeutic purposes, at Notre Dame Child Guidance Clinic in Glasgow (Bowyer, 1970). This was of interest not only for the work described. It was in this clinic that I had been given the opportunity to observe the work of a play therapist. It was there that I had experienced, for the first

---

[1] Bowyer is Ruth Pickford's maiden name.

time, that kind of esoteric atmosphere which can be generated in a room where the mainly non-verbal expression of a child's concerns is being received with sensitivity and understanding.

But of all that was read and remembered, the words which far outweighed the rest came from John Hood-Williams. They were contained in an article in which he outlines the principles underlying the work of the Institute of Child Psychology in London, which was set up and developed by Margaret Lowenfeld through the years 1928 to 1933.

> Nothing quite like this had ever been done before, and the results were surprising. For one thing, many of the children got better. Enuretics ceased wetting their beds, disruptive and unruly children became calmer, asthmatics became symptom-free, children failing at school for lack of concentration became able to concentrate and succeeded at school, withdrawn children became outgoing.
>
> Thus a therapeutic process was clearly seen to be operating, even though none of the classical pre-requisites for psychotherapy was being observed. No interpretations were offered to the children about the unconscious significance of their play; there was no privacy; nor was a transference relationship developed. (Hood-Williams, 1974, pp. 73–4)

There was no reason to doubt the truth of what John Hood-Williams had to say. What part the sand-tray materials might play in achieving this therapeutic effect, and what processes were involved, were questions which demanded consideration throughout the enquiry.

4

GOING UP THE MOUNTAIN BEFORE DESCRIBING THE VIEW

Many of the ideas which influenced the development of the work came from my experience as a nursery school teacher on an island off the west coast of Canada. The school, which was situated at the far end of a Haida Indian village, consisted of a large dilapidated wooden building with two spacious classrooms. I was one of the two 'white' teachers who were employed there.

The day's routines and activities were already well established when I took up the position. They had been set in place by two experienced and well-travelled teachers from England and were generously handed on by the two Haida teacher aides who bridged the changeover in staff. They were employed in the school as part of their training and it was anticipated they would take over responsibility for it on completion of their studies.

My only previous experience of working with very young children had been during my training as a teacher in physical education. This had taken place at a time when there was an emphasis on creative dance and the imaginative use of small and large apparatus, and I found no difficulty in translating some of the basic principles of that discipline into this new and different challenge.

Despite the quality of the regime there were still numerous opportunities to enhance it through the application of one's own particular talents. The rooms were very basic with wooden walls and a floor covered with old linoleum. This meant it was possible to adapt the environment to the children's needs without fear of spoiling the decor. Partitions were constructed and furniture was altered and painted. An extra door in one of the rooms opened up onto a large area of grass and sand and there was much to explore and bring in from outside. The trees along one side of the building extended for more than a mile to the sea, and there was a path which even the smallest children could walk on a good day. Another aspect of the sea could be seen from the top of the steps leading to the main door of the school.

9

It was in this setting that I first began to appreciate the benefits, for both the child and the teacher, of creating an environment in which materials of interest are permanently set out as a backcloth to changing group and individual work activities.

And so it was, many years on, when given the opportunity to spend three weeks in a school of my choice as another part of the Special Needs course, I asked to go to a nursery school. There was one slight drawback: the placement was meant to have a relevance to the course and I was required to have a plan of action. As I remember it now, I was primarily interested in using the time to compare my previous experience in the Haida nursery school with what I would find in this one. Thereafter I would attempt to relate my observations to the work in the child guidance unit. More specifically, I wanted to try out the sand-tray materials with very young children.

My supervisor for this part of the course would have preferred me to be less vague about my intentions and more willing to declare what I hoped to achieve, even before I knew what it was. Again I found myself in a predicament similar to the one I had experienced while waiting for the subject of the dissertation to be revealed. It took several years for me to realise that I approach most creative tasks in this way. I would be less defensive now about asserting my right to uphold that tendency. I do remember trying to explain my dilemma to him over tea and toast in the head teacher's room, during one of several face-to-face encounters we had in the nursery school. I also recall feeling greatly relieved when the words I was searching for came flooding into my mind and I suggested that he surely would not want someone to describe the view from a mountain until they had climbed it.

All the staff in the school, however, appeared to have no difficulty with this stance and were remarkably understanding. I merely explained that I wanted to take my time deciding how best I could help them and myself. When I spoke about the sand-tray materials to the head teacher she responded with genuine interest and gave me all the support and practical help I could have required.

To begin with, I assisted with the never-ending preparation, tidying and cleaning which are the basic activities of life in any good nursery school. This proved to be good training for the work to come. Once I had made arrangements to take the children for singing each day, something which I knew I could do well, I was able to relax a little and concentrate on how best to employ the rest of my time.

On my first day I had joined a group of children outside in the playground and had thrown and caught a ball with a very silent girl, who was also new to the place. She did not speak and her silence was of a kind which prompted me to emulate it. I carried a small book around with me in which to make notes and for a while I thought I might record in detail her progress as she settled in at the school. After several hours of observing her tentatively from a distance, I felt this was a rather intrusive pursuit and abandoned the idea. It would have also become impractical as my other duties increased.

Between the times of general helping, taking singing and presenting the sand tray to individual children, my main occupation was to sit beside them and make certain that materials such as jigsaw puzzles, plasticine, paper, pencils and crayons were available as required.

On one occasion, after being called away to help out elsewhere, I suddenly realised that I had left my notebook and a biro pen lying on a table. When I returned to pick it up I found a very bright, energetic boy about to draw a picture in it. He expected me to intervene by taking away the pen and the notebook and when I asked if he would like to draw a picture in it he was delighted. Other children, noticing what had happened, very quickly gathered round to ask if they could also draw in the book. As it was small, and I was unwilling to have it all used up for this purpose, I let each child draw one picture while I quickly prepared some small pieces of newsprint of a similar size. They were used with just as much enthusiasm. The pages of the book and the pieces of paper were approximately 16 cm x 10 cm.

From that day on the demand for these materials increased rapidly. Whenever I appeared there was an expectation that I would have a pocketful of pens and be carrying a pile of paper. I fulfilled this by buying more pens and by preparing a large supply of paper before each morning and afternoon session. Some of the children stayed for lunch and attended both sessions, but a new group arrived in the afternoon and it was possible to meet as many as 140 different children in one day. As more and more drawings were produced, I noted with particular interest two of the ways in which the children were using them: as a means of communicating with self and others, and as a stimulus to finding the words to express an idea or a concern.

Many of the children who were very reticent about making contact with me through words did so through their drawings. I first became aware of this with the girl with whom I had played ball on the first day. She spent a lot of time sitting beside me drawing pictures but never speaking. I can also recall clearly a very silent boy who frequently came over, drew a picture, then handed it to me with a look which suggested I knew exactly what it meant. I usually received them with a nod. This helped me to overcome the dilemma of wanting to convey to him that I understood their significance, without risking his retreat by revealing my ignorance of the exact nature of their content. I would manage this more honestly now. Very slowly these two acutely shy children began to put words to their pictures. Their first words to me, on completing a series of drawings, were 'me done'. I only made the connection much later in the work, but there was a strong similarity between the manner in which children finished a series of drawings and the way they brought a sand tray, or a series of them, to completion.

Much of the children's pleasure in the drawing undoubtedly came from the amount of undivided attention they were receiving from me. And this was given added weight by the practice of writing the child's name, as well as the date and the time, on the drawing as it was produced. A large part of the attraction came from the biro pen and its association with grown-up writing. More importantly, I think, the pens were enjoyed because they moved easily over the paper and made such clear marks. In my opinion the detail achieved facilitated an increased clarity of expression and improved the communication between the children and their productions. I heard several children cry out in spontaneous delight at some of the images they produced, but of course this may have had nothing to do with the pens.

The whole experience did leave me wondering if the practice was still widespread of providing young children with big pencils and crayons on the assumption that they find them easier to manipulate. Only two children appeared to have any difficulty using a biro pen, but they also had equal difficulty using all sizes of pencils and crayons.

Another factor in the production of the more detailed drawings may well have been the size of the paper itself. So far I have been unable to find any information on the relationship between the dimensions of a piece of paper and what is produced on it, but I assume some must exist.

I drew no profound conclusions from my observations in the nursery. I collected and mounted hundreds of drawings, compiled a list of the subjects and objects depicted in them, and presented them all as the groundwork for a more extensive study at some future time. I did not fool anyone with this. But, as I had to hire a taxi to get them to the college, I think the bulk of material which I handed over made it difficult for those overseeing this aspect of the work to be too critical about my efforts.

Whatever anyone else might have thought of them, I felt quietly certain that the experience had provided me with another of the pieces I needed for the task still to be revealed. And, as I am about to explain, it did. Or I made it do so.

The experience with the drawings in the nursery school prepared the ground for the development of the procedure which came to be called Talk and Draw.

5

Practices and Provisions

Talk and Draw

When I returned to the child guidance unit at the end of the course, I had five children in my group. As a first activity, before they began working on their main class assignments each morning, I introduced the biro pens and small pieces of paper. They took to these with ease. The only problem was a tendency to repeat familiar and well practised images. For some this seemed to be a defence against producing a picture which might be derided. One boy repeatedly drew a picture which had provoked enthusiastic praise from a teacher at his previous school and he kept hoping for more of the same from someone else.

To try to veer the children away from such repetitions I suggested that they do drawings of their thoughts and dreams. Again I was remarkably surprised how easy they all found this. As with the children at the nursery school, the demand for the small pieces of paper was strong. The need to reduce the time spent preparing them was facilitated by the discovery of a large supply of notebooks of plain paper in one of the stockroom cupboards. The pages were almost the same size as the pieces of paper I had been providing. The books were given the title 'Pictures from my Imagination'.

The children usually did one picture each day. The images were mostly of dreams and fantasies, with the occasional reference to a person or incident at home or in the unit. For most of the children the mechanics of writing were a problem, so I wrote any comments they wanted to make on the bottom of the drawing. There were other less burdensome ways for them to practise writing. The books became part of the classwork routine and the drawing of ideas and dreams an accepted feature of the room's culture. Some of the children progressed to producing sequences of drawings in the morning, mostly out of a genuine interest in the activity but sometimes as a ploy to delay the onset of 'real' work.

The development of Talk and Draw was given a significant boost after I had placed a piece of paper between myself and a boy who was upset, in an attempt to concentrate his attention in one place.

14

He succeeded so well in drawing himself out of the mood that I used this procedure with him on numerous other occasions, eventually employing it with others in similar situations. With the first child, a boy called David who will be introduced more formally later, we did very little talking at the start but this increased over the months until the pictures and words were in a better balance.

Before going on the course, my only strategy for leading children away from physically acting out their concerns had been to encourage them to talk. To make this a more focused activity we had a special talking chair for the purpose, positioned in the quietest corner of the room. I usually sat opposite the child and quite close, to keep what was said as confidential as possible. It was helpful with the most distressed children only in dealing with relatively superficial matters. But for many, cultivating the habit of talking through their concerns did bring results in the long term.

Of course, once the role of the chair was understood and accepted, the act of sitting in it, for children who were frightened of the consequences of talking about what troubled them, could be a terror in itself. There were many times when an invitation to sit down and talk sent children running out of the room as fast as they could travel.

Putting the talking with the drawing did not suddenly make it easy for the children to express their concerns but it had distinct advantages over the chair; the contact was much less direct and therefore not so threatening. Once the child's concerns were out there on the paper they could be reappraised, modified and related to anew, and they could even be totally erased. This is a more comfortable process than words leaving the lips and, without further opportunity to exert control, going straight into a grown-up's ear.

At this stage of its development, Talk and Draw was practised on whatever paper was at hand, on any surface available, whenever a child required. It began to be used with such frequency, however, that it became necessary to be better prepared and a permanent site was established. The decision to do this was crystallised by one event in particular.

A special session had been arranged for a girl who needed an opportunity to talk in complete privacy. In preparation for this a large pile of newsprint and a black felt pen had been placed on one of the tables. There was a chair at either side of it. The choice of materials was dictated by a wish to obtain large clear images and by the fact that there was an abundant supply of newsprint in the unit. Although she was undoubtedly ready to do so, the girl was able to communicate the causes of her considerable distress with enough ease to merit their use with other children on subsequent occasions. As Talk and Draw took over, the use of the talking chair just faded away.

The teacher's desk was chosen to be used exclusively for this purpose. It was one of the old-fashioned kind with a good solid surface and drawers down one side. It fitted well into a corner of the room which was nicely separated from the rest of the activities. This meant it could be used with a fair amount of privacy even when there were other children around.

In some respects it would have been desirable to have always had the option of arranging individual sessions, whenever the issues involved were of a very sensitive nature. But too many of them would have interrupted the flow of children coming to the room, and reduced the number who could have made use of it in one day. It was possible, however, to address quite serious issues with other children present. As each child gained experience of using Talk and Draw they became both understanding about its purpose and co-operative about its execution. It was necessary at times to plead for some peace and quiet but it was rare to be seriously interrupted.

Gradually a sort of ritual developed. It was very simple. The child and the worker sat side by side. The same chairs, the same size and type of paper, and the same kind of large felt pen were almost always used. The paper was newsprint approximately 59.4 cm x 42 cm and the pen was usually an Edding 2000. Alongside the drawing, as it was being executed, the worker recorded most of what the child said. The child during this stage of the procedure was in full control of what was written down and could decide to alter or obliterate parts or all of what was produced. Children could use one, several, or, if supplies allowed, as many sheets of paper as they wished in a single session. The most any child used with me was thirty.

When, in the child's estimation, the interaction was complete, the paper was folded twice, placed on a side table and removed from the room at the end of the day. Children were not allowed to take the paper from the room. The issues covered ranged from the slight to the deeply serious and some of the latter were of such a sensitive nature it was felt they would be open to misinterpretation and abuse. As it would have been difficult to make certain only benign material left the premises, the simplest option was not to let any of these productions be taken away. The exception to this was an overriding professional or legal reason relating to the child's welfare. Then, as with any other information which the child brought to the worker, their co-operation was assiduously sought and almost always secured as regards if, how, when, where and with whom it might be shared.

And that was how Talk and Draw came about.

MAKING A TRAY

Again, on my return to the unit I had the choice of installing the sand-tray materials in the classroom I had used before going on the course, or clearing out a similar one and setting them up there. I opted to make a fresh start. By combining the furniture and supplies from both rooms the end result was a well-stocked creative environment with one area kept solely for class work.

This had within it five individual desks for the children, the large teacher's desk (which has already been mentioned and was rarely used by the teacher) and a bookshelf and table for school books and other equipment. Such a limited provision for this aspect of the work meant that, on a practical level if not a philosophical one, the first step in transforming the classroom into a creative facility was achieved with little more than the removal of the children's desks and the replacement of the school supplies with toys and other creative materials.

During my time on the course, apart from introducing the materials to the children in the nursery, I had also used them in a remedial room in a primary school and in a school for children with moderate learning difficulties. My method of presenting them had been strongly influenced by the two lecturers who supervised my work for the dissertation. Added to their anxiety about my trespassing on the territory of educational psychologists were their apprehensions about my indulging in wild interpretive comment of the Kleinian kind. Anxious at the time that such reservations on their part might lead to the total demise of the project, I leapt to the extreme position of saying I would do nothing more than present the materials and observe the response. And this I did. These restrictions, with slight modifications, were to have a major impact on the approach to working with children which was eventually devised.

Once the work was underway in the unit, I felt much freer and gained enough experience to let a way of working take shape which was more closely suited to the children's needs and mine. An intentional lack of detailed knowledge about other methods of tray-making prevents me from placing my own in a wider context. Consequently I will confine myself to describing how it was practised in the room, along with a detailed list of the materials which were in use at the time this study was completed. These were based on the inventory provided by Ruth Pickford in the miraculous leaflet, formally entitled 'Expression of Thoughts'.

> The 'World' material devised by the late MARGARET LOWENFELD of London comprises 300–400 small toys, a tray of rust-proof metal, measuring approximately 75 x 52 x 7 cm, with sand covering the bottom of the tray to a thickness of several centimetres. The toys are arrayed on shelves or in boxes in eight basic categories, as follows: (1) buildings, (2) people, (3) wild animals, (4) domestic animals, (5) trees, bushes, (6) fences, gates, (7) vehicles and (8) a miscellaneous lot of auxiliary objects such as traffic signs, ladders, benches, and small mirrors to depict water. An alternative method for indicating water is to have the bottom of the tray painted blue to represent a lake or ocean when the sand is pushed aside. (Pickford, 1975, p. 188)

My early attempts to find a metal or a plastic tray of the dimensions described above were unsuccessful, and the first tray I used on the course was plastic and approximately 60 cm x 40 cm x 7 cm. As I carried all the materials in a rucksack and travelled by public transport, I tried to ease my load by employing whatever trays were available in the schools I visited. Some of these were even smaller than the one detailed above. It was assumed that there was a special significance in the dimensions of the tray advocated by Margaret Lowenfeld but for the purposes of this study a wide variety of sizes and types were employed. For one child a large glass sweetie jar proved to be an effective 'tray'.

The first tray to be set up in the room, for the specific purpose of tray-making, was a large wooden standing tray. This was approximately 115 cm x 60 cm x 12 cm. There was such a demand for it that it soon became necessary to provide another. This was a strong plastic water tray which was no longer capable of containing water. It measured 90 cm x 50 cm x 10 cm and was placed on a low table in front of one of the windows. They were named, respectively, The Big Tray and The Blue Tray at the Window.

All the trays in use acquired names. The Deepie had once been a large drawer. It was painted blue and was approximately 60 cm x 45 cm x 40 cm. Its name came from the depth of the sand it contained, which was kept at approximately 32 cm. It was an excellent tray in which to bury things. The trays usually had sand to about two-thirds of their depth. Another drawer had come from a bank. This was 50 cm x 30 cm x 20cm, painted white and called The

New Tray. There was also The Baker's Tray – which it had been – measuring approximately 90 cm x 60 cm x 10 cm. And there were two small shallow drawers which had been fitted with carpet. These measured 45 cm x 30 cm x 8 cm and were used mostly for depicting domestic scenes, not always of the most orthodox kind.

The sand in the trays varied in consistency. Apart from those occasions when the children made what they called muddy trays and had a profoundly messy time, their preference was for it to be slightly damp; just enough for it to be easily moulded and shaped. Muddy trays consisted of a mixture of sand and water, usually with the emphasis on the water. The sand in The Dry Tray, which had also been a baker's tray, was so dry that a light dust was created in the air as it was moved around. The eventual number of trays in use was dictated by the need to have a freshly-prepared tray available for every child who entered the room. Apart from those which were used for tray-making there were numerous other smaller trays made of wood and plastic. In these were displayed the various categories of toys and materials.

Everything in the room – the trays, the toys and any other objects – were tried and discarded until only those which had a consistent appeal for the majority of the children remained. The placing of each activity and the arrangement of the materials were also adjusted until they were making their maximum contribution to the room's effectiveness. By the time it had reached its most settled stage, the few changes which continued to be made came from the children's suggestions for new toys and objects. A card on which to write these was kept on a hook by The Blue Tray at the Window. All requests were acquired as soon as money and availability allowed.

The easiest way to illustrate which materials survived the above process is by naming them in the order they would have been encountered in a complete tour of the room:

- Trees and bushes
- Wild animals
- Doll's furniture, wooden and plastic
- Playmobile people and other equipment
- Hospital people and equipment
- People made of different materials and of various sizes and shapes
- Soldiers
- Tanks and army equipment
- Fences and gates
- Roads and bridges

- Domestic animals
- Stones of various kinds and sizes
- Sections of tree branches, with and without bark
- Imitation grass in pieces of various sizes
- String of different strengths and thicknesses
- Houses, buildings and sheds
- Pieces of wood, cut in the shape of flames and painted to look like fire
- Cars, trucks, rescue and construction vehicles
- Small train engines and tenders
- Monsters
- Big animals
- Play dishes and cutlery
- Plastic fruit and eggs
- Alcan foil and cotton wool

Strips of thick cardboard on which were printed the words 'PLEASE DO NOT TOUCH' could be added to the list. These were used with assertive pleasure on numerous occasions but mostly when children were taking a temporary break from their tray to spend time at Talk and Draw. Other strips of cardboard, each with a child's name printed on it, were kept in a holder on one of the walls. Alongside these was another indicating that day's date. These were usually placed down the side of the sand, by the child or the worker, when a tray was completed and before a photograph was taken.

As it was practised in the room, the activity of tray-making involved the selecting, placing and arranging of various toys, objects and materials, in sand which had been moulded into various shapes and contours. Often the children left the sand as it had been prepared for them, slightly rough but level.

Tray productions ranged from those in which no objects were used and there was a minimum of sand construction, to others which could take several hours to complete, involved complex sand-formations and structures, and incorporated scores of objects and other materials. Water, in containers or simulated with materials such as blue paper or Alcan foil, featured frequently in the trays. Glass mirrors were never used, for safety reasons, although in retrospect I think more shiny materials of a safe kind should have been provided.

Once a child had established a comfortable familiarity with the activity of tray-making (which for many of them took only a few seconds) they were usually asked if they would like to say something about it. Great care was taken to assure that they felt completely at ease about saying nothing. Many were unpractised in politely deflecting or refusing to answer a question from an adult. To help them overcome this inexperience, the phrase 'there's no story' was offered until they were ready to find one for themselves. As the words which accompanied the tray constructions were rarely in the form of a story it was not particularly apt; however, as it initially came from the children and seemed to meet their requirements, no attempt was ever made to change it. It was a phrase which was taken up by most of the children. Another favoured comment was, 'It's private'. The very careful support of the children's right to refuse or to avoid comment about a production meant that any talking they decided to do was very much on their own terms.

Once a tray had been completed, responded to and photographed, it was usually dismantled by the worker, but only with the child's consent.

Several activities emerged as the main complements to tray-making. They were painting, making objects with clay and constructing with cardboard boxes and all kinds and qualities of cardboard and paper.

Boxes require a special mention as they fulfilled several functions. There were not enough toys for everyone who used the room to have a separate collection, so each child, usually after their first visit, came to town with me and bought a small object of their choice. These were kept in the room in a specially selected box or drawer. The boxes employed for this purpose included red plastic elastoplast boxes, a cedar wood box with a faded picture and words about friendship on the lid and small white cardboard boxes. These were popular because they could be decorated.

Other boxes – some small, many large, best plain, white and brown – were in constant demand for a different purpose. I have no proof of this, but those children who were known to have been sexually abused appeared to be using them to represent the inside and outside of their bodies. Influenced by their interest, I decided to make every effort to obtain a regular supply.

The response to these from nearly all the children was surprising. I was rarely able to meet the demand and at times had to resort to using boxes and plastic containers with brand names on the outside. I got these in large black plastic bags from the local medical centre. In conjunction with paper, cardboard, glue and staples, they were used to make all kinds of constructions. These ranged from the quite ordinary, such as houses, stables, cars and cameras, to the more extraordinary which could consist of numerous boxes joined together in odd alignment and adorned with misshapen appendages.

The supply of cardboard and paper in the room was usually abundant. I had understood for a long time that different sizes and qualities can be a lively stimulus to drawing and painting. Much of this material had been discarded outside a local printer's and was obtained free of charge.

A large table was permanently set up for clay work and painting. The clay was kept in a plastic bucket on the floor and children were able to take what they needed without assistance. Two white boards on which to work were kept alongside the bucket. There were tools for the clay on the shelves behind the table. The materials for painting were kept on the same shelves. Paint, paper, water and brushes were laid out ready for use almost all of the time. The majority of paintings were done on sugar paper sized approximately 59 cm x 42 cm.

THE ROOM

The sorting process which was used on the materials was also applied to the furniture. I want to describe the pieces which survived along with some of the features of the room which never changed. This is intended to create a physical context for the ensuing words and deeds. It should also give a fuller picture of what would be required to set up a similar facility.

The room itself was approximately 7 m x 5 m. Opposite the only door, on the long east wall, there were three large windows. These provided a view of trees behind which could be seen the low buildings of a community centre. Another window in the centre of the north wall looked out over an overgrown school garden and an inhospitable concrete playground. There were times when both areas were cleared and tidied up but this usually did not last for long. Beyond them was a landscape of industrial buildings and high-rise flats.

At their cleanest and freshest, the walls of the room were pale pink. I had bribed the painters to get them that colour. I chose it to please me and to complement the wood of the furniture and the various rugs and covers which I had brought in. A strong influence on the choice of rugs was their capacity to contain sand. Where the floor was not hidden by them it showed as well-worn red linoleum, faded with age.

The six tables in the room were strong. They were old tables, some with shortened legs, varying in height from 50 cm to 65 cm. Each had a specific use. Three were used to support sand trays. The working surface of the largest table was approximately 2 m x 1 m and, with my help, had been stripped and varnished by the children to give it a good surface. This was the table which was used for the painting and clay work.

There was a low table with a strong wooden box on top situated alongside the large wooden standing tray. I had to climb on them both, to get the height I needed, to take photographs of the children's large tray constructions. The other large table was used mostly for the more messy activities like making muddy trays. There was no supply of water in the room and it was usually carried in an old kettle from a line of sinks which were situated several yards from the door.

Under this table there was a big wooden storage box on wheels measuring approximately 31 cm (depth) x 91 cm (length) x 46 cm (breadth). It had been fitted with a foam base and there was usually a blanket in it. It was emptied on several occasions and used as a very deep tray but usually children climbed in, with or without a feeding bottle, and asked to be covered over with the blanket.[2]

Apart from the big desk which was used for Talk and Draw there was one other large piece of furniture. This was 'the cabin'. I cannot remember how it got its name but it was really a pretend car which had been made by putting a roof of plywood on an upturned table. Its sides had been made by nailing thicker wood onto the legs. A space had been left for a door. A shelf which was supposed to be a dashboard had been constructed inside at the front. Inserted into this was the cross spar of a large pram, with one of the wheels still attached. It had a white rubber rim and acted as a steering wheel. Two firm cushions at the back made up the driver's seat. It was used as a vehicle in which to travel the world, as a place for eating and drinking and, when it was covered over with a blanket or large pieces of cardboard, a place to hide. There were several of these in the room. Somewhere to hide had been identified, by the play therapist at the Notre Dame clinic, as an essential feature of any therapy room.

There were also a number of chairs and stools of different sizes. The two biggest chairs were capable of accommodating a worker and a small child side by side. One of these was the talking chair, which after the introduction of Talk and Draw had reverted to being just a good

---

[2] The use which children made of feeding bottles will be addressed in Part Two.

chair to sit in. And there were also numerous cupboards and shelves, with and without doors, for the storage and display of materials.

As regards the overall nature of such a facility, it should fulfil two basic criteria. The worker should like the space, be comfortable with its dimensions and feel able, albeit with a struggle at times, to encompass everything that might happen there. For the children, when they stand at the door of the room for the very first time, they should see before them a place which is immediately recognisable, on some level, as having been prepared with the greatest of care especially for their purposes.

FINAL PREPARATIONS

From the moment the sand-tray materials were introduced to the children in my group they were used with great enthusiasm and tray-making soon became an integral feature of the day's activities.

For the first few weeks I doggedly adhered to the established discipline of completing class assignments before moving on to any other creative activities. I was reluctant to let go of a routine which could be as useful as a means of settling the children each morning as it was for improving their academic performance. Incidentally, visitors to the unit often failed to appreciate the sense of security which can be engendered, for both the child and the worker, by the systematic working-through of an adequately challenging set of workbooks.

As the demand for sand trays increased and was met, the space for school work became more cramped. The children continued to begin the day by drawing in the books 'Pictures from my Imagination', but as some of them began to come into the room in the morning declaring they had an important idea for a tray, and I was unable think of a good reason for not letting them proceed with it, the practice of following the drawing with class work was broken. And then, for children who were feeling particularly upset or unable to settle to work, spending time with a tray seemed like a perfectly reasonable way to begin the day.

Because the demand for trays was never allowed to exceed the provision, it was possible to develop a flexible and mostly amicable regime as regards when trays could be made and school work should get done.

It was accepted practice in the unit for children to make visits to other classes during the afternoon sessions. These could be for social reasons alone, or to join in a group activity which was being offered by a particular teacher on that day. Children began to visit my room to make trays and it was the seriousness of the concerns being expressed in these, and in their drawings, which initiated the change in its function and my role in it.

There was no clean break from one use to another. The whole transition from classroom to special facility took place over a period of several months and was geared mainly to the readiness of the children in my group to move on. Three of them joined other groups within the unit. Two boys who had been scheduled to do so went on to residential schools.

By the time the changeover was well in hand my ideas about how the room should be managed, in relation to the rest of the unit, were clearly formulated. They were based directly on the practices which had developed around the use of the sand trays in my classroom. The children would be given as much control and responsibility over when they could visit the room as was feasible within the organisation of their particular class. With the teachers who were sympathetic to the work, a child would be required to say little more than, 'I've got an idea for a tray', or, 'I have something I want to sort out.'

The length of time a child remained with me would reflect the intensity of their involvement in any of the activities available. Included in these would be the more nebulous preoccupations of being in the no-man's-land between the need to talk and fear of doing so. The decision to adopt this regime was based initially on the simple observation that the time children took to complete a tray satisfactorily could vary greatly.

As regards bringing visits to a comfortable conclusion, there was never any situation which could not be managed with a mixture of common sense and a little ingenuity. On the whole the children became well aware of how long they should be in the room and understood that, with others waiting, it was only fair to leave when their particular task, or tasks, had been completed. Children who were going through an acutely distressing period were sometimes allowed to remain in the room for a whole morning or afternoon, and very occasionally for a day. The situations which required most sensitivity were probably those when a child, no longer engrossed in any particular activity, was, on an unconscious level, holding on to the room's nourishing attributes. As moving them on in such circumstances was akin to weaning, it was vital to ease them very gently on their way.

My experience with the original five boys had given me a rough idea of how many children I could comfortably manage at one time. With four class groups in the unit, and a maximum of six children in each, it was decided that the average number of children in the room at any given time would be one from each of the groups. It was necessary to be flexible about this as sometimes two children from one group were in need of a visit whilst there would be no one from another.

There were several mismanaged occasions when as many as eight children were present at one time. This could be exciting on one level but was unsustainable, as far as my resources were concerned, for longer than about half an hour. Such times were, of course, balanced by the quieter ones when children were being helped on an individual basis. These sessions, in spite of the reservations expressed earlier, had increased in frequency by the end of the project.

There is no doubt that I began this work with unrealistic expectations. I genuinely believed that, as soon as its potential benefits became apparent to others, any initial reservations would fade away and the help required for its development, both inside and outside the unit, would be quickly forthcoming.

It took me a long time to understand that only on rare occasions can the personalities of adults be subdued sufficiently to keep focused on the task in hand, even when that task is to alleviate the distress of young children. And of course I include my own personality in this.

I remain convinced, however, that the management of the facility within the unit was as easy, or as difficult, as the adults involved wanted it to be.

Part II

Seeking Direction

6

First Steps

From the time I had discovered the leaflet to the time I sat down to write up the work, six years had passed.

Throughout that period I had taken photographs of almost every sand tray, every clay object and anything else which the children had produced. I had also photographed some of the paintings and drawings, although usually these were kept in a safe place in the room where they could be referred to if required. The photographic evidence which accumulated was extensive. On some days I took over fifty photographs. I handed them in for processing after work, collected them the following day and shared them with the children on day three. Many of these were of individual features of the tray constructions and for a long time I took two exposures of each tray so that the children could have a copy. I had to stop this because of the expense.

By the time I was settled in the room I had finished experimenting with different cameras and tripods and with finding ways to get high enough above a tray to get a relatively undistorted view of the construction. I had opted for a Pentax 35 mm single-lens reflex and, as indicated earlier, was getting all the height I needed by standing on tables and boxes. With four large windows the room was usually quite bright. In the darkest days of winter the photographs acquired an orange tinge from the fluorescent lighting but it was always possible to obtain a readable print of what the children had made.

The extent to which the presence of the camera in the room was an influence on the children's response to me and the materials was tested out superficially during the last six months of the project. I stopped taking photographs completely and left the camera at home. In some respects I may have missed it more than the children did. Apart from a further reduction in photographic costs, and a lessening of pleasure for one boy who had a very strong aesthetic appreciation of his own tray productions, I was unable to detect any obvious changes in how the room functioned. As regards the more subtle ones – and I am certain there must have been many – they would have been too difficult to identify with the naked eye.[3]

---

[3] Further comment on the function of the camera in the room is made in Chapter 15: 'A Remarkable Container'.

I had made frequent use of the same camera in the nursery school in Canada where I had taken hundreds of photographs of the children. These were mainly portraits and pictures of their involvement in group activities, and they were used as a means of reflecting back to them who they were and what they were achieving. Through that experience I had reached a stage where the camera was more an extension of me than an object with a separate function. My familiarity with it may well have contributed to its acceptance by the children; as might my open declaration that I was taking the photographs and keeping records to get a better understanding of what troubled them, and how I might best help them to get things sorted out. The only real difficulty I had with it was on the few occasions when a child picked it up and ran around the room in a desperate attempt to get my attention. The ploy usually succeeded. Otherwise they treated it with tenderness.

For most of the study I used white index cards to record the children's spoken words and to keep the photographs in some sort of order. I mounted the photograph on one card and copied out the verbal comments on another. I transferred these each evening from the notebook which I employed in the room during the day. At a later stage I changed to using files as this enabled me to put the children's words directly onto file paper while I was in the room. I left a space at the top of each page for the photograph to be inserted later. This took less time but I think I lost a lot by not reappraising what the children had said in the rewriting process.

I turned continually to these records in my efforts to understand what the children were trying to achieve with the materials. I used them as a sieve through which to put all the various theories and ideas I subsequently encountered or contrived.

As the practical work gained momentum, it propelled me faster and deeper into a local university library. I had dipped in there briefly on numerous occasions during my studies for the dissertation, but now I was taking more of a plunge into what was virtually an unknown sea, with no clear idea of where I might eventually come ashore. I do not wish to give the impression here of someone setting out alone to find their own path to psychotherapeutic enlightenment. I had made several attempts to find institutional shelter. Included in these was an application to the Scottish Institute of Human Relations. I had aspirations of establishing a firm theoretical base from which to proceed with the practical work. Unfortunately, at the time none of the courses available related to work with children, and I was considered to be ineligible for the analytic psychotherapy course, for lack of adult practice, if nought else. I also began to study for a degree in psychology but became convinced after several months that it would be unable to provide me with what I was looking for.

With no formal supervision, academic or otherwise, I really had no alternative but to rely for guidance almost totally on what the children did and what some writers said. In many respects I think I was fortunate in having to find my own way, but the disadvantages of being outside the system are only marginally compensated for by the joys of feeling free to go anywhere.

Most of my reading came from the books and journals which were available in that one library. It was supplemented by those I bought and those I requested from the British Library. The high cost of these sometimes discouraged me from obtaining all the material I thought might be useful. It could be argued that, if I had been able or willing to spend more, I would have ended up making entirely different assumptions from those about to be offered here.

There was one incident during the course of the work which proved to have implications both for the work's progress and for me personally. It may also have had theoretical repercussions by making me cleave with added fervour to psychodynamic theory, as one might to a loved and perniciously maligned parent. It will be considered later in relation to its influence on the outcome of the work, but for the time being it is introduced in respect of its effect on the writing-up process.

Suffice to say that it left me with a rather distorted perspective of how a paper on the work might be received by others and, as a consequence, I attempted to produce a rather formal account. This was intended to draw any anticipated criticism firmly towards the ideas and away from me personally. As part of that same misguided strategy I also decided to keep any mention of my contribution, as the worker, to a minimum.

Not surprisingly, the first comments I received from those who read the early drafts were that it did not provide enough information about my interaction with the children. But by that time I had already started writing a series of complementary papers which were intended to remedy this deficiency. Three of these are presented in Part Three: 'Companions on the Way'. There was no doubt that I hoped eventually to be able to share the work with others, but I did not attempt to take this to the logical conclusion of tailoring what I wrote for possible publication. I used the process almost exclusively as a means of trying to make sense of all that had been happening in the room.

The result of that effort was entitled 'Externalising the Unpleasurable, First Steps Towards a Symbolic Reconstruction'. In the version to be presented here, the original introduction has been removed. The majority of the issues which it covered have now been incorporated into Part One of this book, otherwise the text remains virtually unchanged in tone and content.

7

THREE EARLY ENCOUNTERS

Once the room had been set up as a facility within the unit it soon became obvious that one of the primary needs of the children was to find some form of expression for what will be referred to for the moment as the negative elements and aspects of their experience. There had been indications of this need in some of the earliest encounters with individual children.

One boy, who had sworn his way to rejection in previous placements, seemed intent on doing the same in this one. His behaviour was viewed as a superficial manifestation of some very serious problems, but it set a raucous expectation as regards swearing and was influential in deciding what the children would be allowed to do in the room.

The swearing gradually calmed down, as he did, but through his need to have it received and understood, 'getting out swearies' became, with certain evolving qualifications, an acceptable form of expression within the room. As swearing was conceived of as bad by children, and declared as such by adults, it was felt that an extravagant but structured opportunity to swear might help facilitate the expression, or release, of other conceived of 'bad things'.

This explanation of why swearing was allowed was given to the children whenever it was considered necessary or helpful. They rarely failed to understand; adults frequently did.

In a second encounter, in a slow and distressing lead-up to a disclosure of sexual abuse by her father, a girl took up this phrase, adapted it for her own purposes and for many weeks could speak only of a need to 'get out her worries'. During this time she expressed her concerns symbolically, in stories, pictures and trays, until she was able to find the words and felt safe enough to describe what had been happening to her.[4] For ever after this she used the phrase 'I'm getting out my worries', sometimes abbreviated to just 'worries', as a means of indicating whenever she was even slightly upset and in need of help.

---

[4] Several of the tray stories she told are presented in Part Four.

Both of these phrases, 'getting out swearies' and 'getting out worries', and variations of them, were taken up by almost all of the children and used as an everyday means of declaring that they had something troubling them. The frequency of their use was, for some time, overwhelming. This was a characteristic of many of the early, universally appropriated, responses to the environment.

The third encounter relates to a boy who spent an hour in the room one morning making trays before quietly, and seemingly comfortably, returning to his class group. At lunchtime, in the dining-room, with the approval of his teacher, he came over to demonstrate with his hand that from the top of his head to his toes he was full of worries. He said, 'they have been dragging me down for a long time', and added that he wanted to get them out immediately.

We went directly to the room where he drew, and talked about the nightmares which had been troubling him since the death of his grandfather.[5] He said he hadn't spoken of this before, or about how he often cried at night when he was alone in bed. Having talked this over, apparently to his satisfaction, he suggested he'd like to make a tray. He proceeded to do so, then interrupted the task to come over to the big desk, scrawl enthusiastically all over a sheet of newsprint, and say 'This is all my worries I'm getting out. I'm covering the page. That's it.' He then returned to his class for the second time that day. Several days later he said that his nightmares had got very small and had then disappeared.

This kind of impromptu visit, resulting in at least a partial resolution of some of the child's difficulties, was just one of many which were made in similar circumstances. It was a crucial factor in the decision to provide the children with a substantial measure of control over when they could visit the room. It was also to become one of the most contentious, as well as one of the most important, features of the work.

---

[5] The series of drawings produced during this visit are included in the examples of Talk and Draw in Part Four.

8

'DAVID'

The need to give expression to negative aspects of experience had also been evident in the work with David, who was the first child to have access to the room and the materials every day, throughout the day, and who had taken to them with relief and much abandon. David was ten years old, and almost totally out of control, when he joined my group.

He had previously been erratically controlled through the threat that he would be punished by his father if he behaved badly. The fear of his father's wrath was both real and phantasied. When my work with David began, the involvement of his father in the management of the case was reduced to a minimum, and then stopped entirely. This was to give David the opportunity to begin to take control and be responsible for his own difficulties. Because of the extreme destructiveness of some of his outbursts, however, it was made clear to him that if at any time he became a serious risk to himself or to others, his father might need to be contacted. It was stressed repeatedly that the preferred approach was to try to work out everything, there, with him, in the room. This threat was purposefully but reluctantly employed on several very extreme occasions, as a means of re-establishing safe contact and control with David. Its use was totally rescinded as the risk reduced and the relationship progressed.

To begin with, David's distress could not be contained by the materials or the environment, and at times he had to be held physically to prevent damage to himself or to others.[6]

The most acute and disturbing issue for him concerned the murder of the woman who had lived with them for several years. David had been present in the house on the night she had been killed by his father. His own mother had left the family home when he was about four years old.

Allied to this was the overwhelming feeling that his life was in a total mess. Whilst his father had been in prison, he had spent several

---

[6] There is more about this and other aspects of the work with David in Part Three.

35

unsettled and disrupted years in children's homes. For much of the time he had been unable to sustain attendance at any kind of school.

One of the many ways in which he tried to rid himself of these experiences and feelings was by making messes, both overtly and secretly, with any materials available at the moment his distress became intolerable.

Interestingly, he made a complete mess of only one of more than a hundred trays which he produced over an eighteen-month period. The receiving of the messes, and the gradual and mutual acceptance of them, as an externalised representation of how he felt inside about himself and his life, provided the bridge we both needed until he could achieve a more constructive means of expression. A profusion of memories and remembered details surrounding the night of the murder and subsequent related events gradually surfaced, mostly in sequences of drawings. Sometimes as many as thirty pictures were produced in one uninterrupted flow, and talking about past and present difficulties, both in conjunction with and separately from the drawings, became an integral part of the day's interaction and routine. Much of what he said was directly received by writing it down at the time. This proved to be an effective means of assisting him in the verbal expression of his concerns.

As David became freer and easier in his ability to appraise and talk over the difficulties in his life, so his exploration of the materials in the room intensified and his creative capacity seemed to increase. The messes reduced in frequency and then disappeared. At his most creative, the quality of flow which had been evident in his drawings was also present in his use of the other means of expression available to him, and in his movement between them. With these observations came the first awareness of the possible benefits of creative flow and creative activity in the loosening up of anything in need of expression and release.

It was not until most of David's acute concerns had found some form of expression that he was able to become genuinely interested in class work and begin to take in information and to learn.

9

Themes, Features and Details

Apart from those experiences which found easy and immediate expression through the activity of Talk and Draw, the most effective medium for receiving the children's negative experience was undoubtedly the sand tray. Once it had been expressed in there, its presence was believed to be evident in the individual details of the constructions, and in the various common themes and features which began to be identified. As any discussion of children's symbolic activity is essentially speculative, the following comments will be no exception.

There had been indications, through such features as rescuing and tending to a woman doll, and bringing a doctor to a dying woman, that David may have been attempting to deal with issues relating to the murder on a symbolic level in the sand tray. He made no direct connections between the productions and the event, and none was sought or suggested.

Based on information provided by the child, or by an adult familiar with the child's experiences, there were numerous examples of tray constructions in which an easy if unprovable connection could be made between a feature and a real-life event. In one of these, a boy, using toys to represent the main protagonists, played out an incident in which his father had punched and broken his mother's nose.

In another, three children, at different times, had re-enacted aspects of the events surrounding the death of a child from their nursery school, who had been knocked down and killed in a road accident several weeks before.

In a tray in which the real experience was just barely distanced from the production, a boy, using a plastic toy eagle, a nest made of string, and plasticine eggs, reconstructed and then acted-through a frightening incident which had occurred the previous day. As he had been approaching a nest containing eggs, two large black crows had swooped down towards his head and attacked him.

And, in an example of an anticipated event, the day before a hospital appointment to have a vertical scar at his hairline cut and resewn for cosmetic purposes, a boy produced a scene in which a

37

figure, axe in hand, was about to strike a vertical blow, mirroring the real scar, and split open the forehead of another figure. This medical procedure had been resisted by the doctor and the boy, and insisted on by the mother.

These examples, in which connections surfaced without any effort on the part of the worker, were assumed to represent only a small percentage of the many in which negative issues were finding expression in the details of the constructions. It was anticipated that this premise would be clearly confirmed once a better understanding of the children's symbolic language had been achieved.

Whilst the emphasis so far has been on the expression of the negative elements of experience, two major constructive themes, which proved to be central to the children's symbolic intentions, were first recognised in David's work. They were termed 'The Need For Nourishment' and 'Reconstructing The Landscape'. They retained their relevance and were unmodified for the rest of the enquiry. Their presence in David's trays were taken as evidence of his constructive intentions and can be illustrated by some of the words which accompanied his productions.

Everything which David produced could be roughly divided into two main categories: the negative in content; and the constructive in intent, and both appeared in changing measure during all the phases of his use of the room. The comments which are presented here have been selected from all the trays he ever made and are given in chronological order. Each one comes from a different tray.

'It's the desert.'

'It's a wee shopping thing and they're going to be testing the ground to see if it's good to make houses in it.'

'The boat has got stuck on a rock.'

'In the next one the boat's gonnae be out here – it gets moved.'

'The tree's starting to grow everywhere now and all the fences are coming away.'

'The boat, they managed to get it out.'

'They were making all the land different and they made a wee river and they built shops. And they moved away all the old buildings and that.'

'Oh, ah, there's the wee panda, it's eating its leaves.'

'They've made a new land and they've put new animals in it.'

'Look at the road I'm making.'

'I'm making it a tree land.'

'That was the new land they were making.'

'That's a wee land. Hod on I'll put a wee guy having something to eat.'

'Just a normal wee land.'
'It's a wee country road.'

'It's just a wee land wi' a wee river in it. He's trying to get his food leaping about.' [The 'he' is a frog.]

'It's just a seaside. That wee guy's pointing to him and saying my wee boat's better than your wee boat.

It could be argued that any positive or constructive feature in David's work represented more of a wished-for state than an existing one, but it is worth noting that the increase in the more ordered and constructive elements in his trays occurred alongside more settled behaviour and improved relationships, both inside and outside the unit.

As the work progressed and there was a substantial increase in the number of trays being made, it became possible to set what David had been producing into a wider context and begin to identify some common negative themes and features. A more extensive appraisal of all the recorded material will be necessary before firmer categories than those presented here can be devised, but probably the most common and frequently appearing scenario was one in which people, animals and objects were being bitten, eaten or devoured, mainly by other animals or monsters, and sometimes by people. It was given the name 'Biting and Devouring'. Words from R. E. Money-Kyrle seem particularly apt for this theme. In his paper 'An inconclusive contribution to the theory of the Death Instinct' he suggests: 'To every organism another organism has three basic potential meanings. It is something to eat (or reject), something to be eaten by, or something to unite (or reunite) with' (Money-Kyrle,

[1955] 1977, p. 503). And Max Schur, in 'The Ego And The Id In Anxiety' also has something to say on the subject: 'Another ubiquitous danger encountered in every analysis is the danger of being devoured' (Schur, 1958, pp. 213–14).

'Chaos and Confusion' could be present in part of the tray or throughout it. It could be there from the beginning of a production or it could appear at any time, anywhere and to any extent, as the work proceeded. A continual interchange and balance between order and disorder would then ensue, which, at its most unconstructive, would result in a total disorganised mess.

'Situations of Conflict' ranged from formalised battles between evenly balanced and distributed armies, to very unequal encounters between varying numbers of individuals and groups. Again, these were of people, animals and monsters. Also included were 'baddies' of assorted dispositions. Eternal triangles and classic one-to-one confrontations between diverse adversaries were frequently depicted.

In 'Dealing with Dangerous Elements', people, animals and objects were loosely, or excessively, restricted, usually by being walled in, fenced, or barricaded. This was achieved by a variety of materials, ranging from a piece of paper to a mountain of stones. More extreme measures included burial, blasting or obliteration by a variety of procedures, with regurgitation, resuscitation and resurrection available as desired.

Of the many subsidiary themes (too many to be considered here, and some which may have a significance not yet fully appreciated), two were dominant. They were also similar in the sense of threat and unease which they conveyed.

In 'Anxiety Situations' the fear or the actuality of falling, drowning or dying, by various means, was central to the production. An ambulance or a fire engine, and sometimes a rescue helicopter, was either the main participant in the action or was standing by in a state of readiness.

In 'Intruders', one or several creatures, which even before placement might be loosely described as disturbing, were introduced into landscapes of a quite normal or ordinary kind at various times throughout a production. Apart from all kinds of 'baddies' and monsters, some of the more habitual visitors were the witch, the ghost, the skeleton, the alligator and the snake.

There was also a collection of symbolic features which would be difficult to place under one heading. (The word 'feature', as it is being used here, implies an assemblage of several small toys, objects or other materials in close association with each other.) They proved to be of major significance to the work. Although diverse in formation, the characteristics they had in common were a tendency towards persistent and repeated appearances and a marked resistance to change and resolution. The exceptions to this were the occasions when, after a brief or momentary absence, they were replaced by an alternative but essentially similar feature. There were several kinds.

Some had a bizarre or unusual quality which was suggested mainly through an incongruous combination or juxtaposition of objects. An example would be a naked man doll wearing a crash helmet, balanced over the side of a tray, with his feet in a container of plastic eggs.

A second group were more of a conglomeration of objects interlocked and piled up on each other at various angles. When monsters were included in the arrangement, their mouths were often used to hold it all together.

Third were those which would fit in equally well with the theme of biting and devouring. A typical gathering would be a small animal encircled, and being chewed at the edges, by a well-positioned pack of wild animals.

From the earliest awareness of the existence of these features, they were conjectured to be some form of external symbolic representation of internal formulations of a particularly potent or distorted nature. They were later surmised to have been acquired as a consequence of one, several, or an accumulation of extremely negative experiences.

Two other symbolic features considered to be of major significance were 'Getting out the Monsters', and 'Making the Mound'.

'Getting out the Monsters' was really more of an event than a feature. All, or nearly all, of the creatures designated as monsters by the children were very purposefully selected and placed in a tray in which the sand had not been touched or moulded in any way. Each monster was positioned in a distinct space, having no direct contact or relationship with any other. This could take place after several visits, or, as happened with David, after a year of working through acute issues. Its function, until proved otherwise, was seen as a formal and possibly ritualistic symbolic externalising of monstrous (bad) objects. The tray most frequently used for this purpose was the largest and strongest in the room.

The mounds varied in size, structure and complexity. They ranged from a rough pile of sand put together in a few seconds to a carefully formed construction in which, on the surface or deep inside, a diversity of materials, cavities and tunnels had been incorporated. Such a mound might take over an hour to make.

Mounds appeared frequently in all the children's sand-tray productions, and did so mostly in the guise of hills, mountains, volcanoes, sandcastles, pies and sometimes cakes. They were thought capable of expressing the negative or the constructive aspects of a child's experience, depending on their formation and the context in which they appeared.

The possible symbolic significance of the mound was considered initially in connection with a boy who had visited the room almost daily over a period of several months. He only ever made one mound on each visit and would often just sit there contemplating it, in what seemed like a mood of quiet but intense bewilderment. Occasionally he would sprinkle it with sand, or toss things like a small plastic car in its direction. Sometimes he would adorn it with such objects as a big felt hen or a pile of green metal fences. One was given a cotton-wool mouth and then turned into a mouse.

It was known that he had failed to satisfactorily negotiate his mother's breast, or a bottle, and that he'd had persistent feeding and eating difficulties throughout his life. Based on these and associated observations, his relationship with the mound was surmised to represent an extremely confused attempt to symbolically re-negotiate the breast.

The conditions which had been set as regards interpretation became conveniently compatible with the growing conviction that the children's symbolic work (with certain exceptions) should be allowed to proceed in peace. This point of view underpinned the decision not to respond overtly to the details of the children's tray constructions at the time of their appearance.

There were two other main reasons for not doing so. With the environment available to all the children in the unit, an abundance of sand trays were being produced. As a result, the practical considerations involved in just receiving and recording them, apart from attending to everything else which was happening in the room, meant that focusing on the general themes and features became a more feasible option. The other factor was my lack of understanding of the symbolic significance of the details of the constructions. As speculating about them was recognised as a means of remedying this deficiency, however, I did so within the room in silence and outside it, by relying on the photographic records, with enthusiasm.

The extent to which the various common symbolic themes and features were capable of reflecting, and providing a means of monitoring, change in the child's internal disposition became an issue of increasing interest and consideration. Any alteration or transformation of them, extending to their disappearance and reappearance, as well as any overall tendency towards an increase or decrease in the negative or constructive elements, began to be used as a rough guide to the child's progress, or lack of it.

10

FROM NO BREAST TO NO BREAKFAST

The talking and drawing, which had played such an important part in the work with David, had slowly evolved into the more formal and structured activity which has been referred to as Talk and Draw. Once established, it became in its own right, and in the special relationship it developed with the sand tray, central to the approach which was beginning to take shape.

The specific value and function of all the other materials in the room will not be addressed here, although each one, as separate components and in combination, was considered essential to the general effectiveness of the environment.

In the sand-tray constructions it was assumed that the issues being symbolically represented related mainly to experience about which the children were not consciously aware, and indeed might never be. By contrast, in Talk and Draw, the majority of what was being revealed was concerned with incidents and experiences which were readily available to conscious recall.

Moving between these two contrasting forms of expression was thought to be a stimulus to spontaneity and creativity. The sand tray seemed to function like a kind of psychic warm-up for the offloading of conscious concerns through the pictures and words.

Included in the immense range of experiences which were made known through the activity of Talk and Draw were many stories which had been waiting to be told for a long time. There were tales of discovered lies, stolen toys, wet beds, lost dogs and dead fathers, and however serious they were, or were perceived to be, they all had one thing in common: at the time of their happening they had produced at the very least an intensely disturbing effect on the child.

This was illustrated by an incident described by a boy who had felt acute anguish at not having been given any breakfast that morning. He accompanied his account of what had happened with a picture of an armless child.

This very immediate and direct expression of a recent experience has been referred to in the title of this section, alongside the more profound and long-term difficulty of the boy with the mound, as a means of suggesting the breadth and depth of issues seeking expression within the room.

11

THE UNPLEASURABLE

Finding the words to define what was happening in the room became an important part of the process of trying to understand it. The word which came adequately to describe and convey all that the children seemed most in need of expressing was 'unpleasurable'. As I had not read 'Beyond the Pleasure Principle' (Freud, [1920] 1955), and related papers by Freud, at the time the word was probably gleaned from other writers commenting on them. It was used initially because it sounded right. Whilst no attempt was made to place it within any particular theoretical context or framework, once it had been adopted something of its auspicious origins and why it had seemed so apt began to be appreciated.

It had become increasingly apparent that much of the experience which was being revealed by the children was consistent with that which Ernst Kris, in reference to 'shock trauma', calls 'a single experience, when reality powerfully and often suddenly impinges on the child's life' (Kris, 1956, p. 72). Or again in his words, in reference to 'strain trauma', 'the effect of long-lasting situations, which may cause traumatic effects by the accumulation of frustrating tensions' (ibid., p. 73).

The first definition would be applicable to an incident such as the two black crows attacking the boy's head, and the second to the child whose early feeding had been persistently unsatisfactory.

The connection which was being made between trauma and what had been unpleasurable for the children is perhaps more amply accommodated by the definition of trauma provided by S. S. Furst in the opening chapter of *Psychic Trauma,* in which he suggests: 'At the extreme, almost any unpleasant experience or state has been designated as a trauma, particularly if it could be correlated with an adverse psychological effect, either at the time of its occurrence or at some later date' (Furst, 1967, p. 31).

And, in the same chapter, commenting on the terms 'traumatic situation' and 'anxiety trauma' as used by Freud in 'Inhibitions, Symptoms and Anxiety', ([1926] 1959) Furst introduces an issue which was to prove crucial to the evolving understanding of the

45

children's purposes. He speaks of 'experiences of nonsatisfaction and helplessness in which amounts of stimulation rise to unpleasurable heights and cannot be discharged or mastered psychically' (Furst, 1967, p. 13).

It was this unmastered psychic material which seemed to be at the heart of everything the children were seeking to externalise in one form or another. Once this notion had been contemplated a series of related concepts, believed to enhance and support it, came tumbling after.

Charles Rycroft, again in a definition of trauma, refers to 'any totally unexpected experience which the subject is unable to assimilate' (Rycroft, 1972, p. 170). The emphasis here, of course, is on the inability to assimilate. It ties in with a statement in *Play, Dreams and Imitation in Childhood* in which Jean Piaget, writing of 'Certain games (which we called symbolic games of liquidation)', describes them as: 'symbolic productions of painful experiences' which have 'the sole aim of digesting them and assimilating them' (Piaget, 1951, p. 149). And continuing in the same vein, Harry Guntrip, commenting on ideas of Wilfred Bion, writes 'bad experiences cannot be *digested* and absorbed; they are retained as foreign objects which the psyche seeks to project' (Guntrip, [1952] 1968, p. 22).

It was with such words as 'unassimilated', 'undigested' and 'unabsorbed', that 'the unpleasurable' was thought to reside.

12

EXTERNALISING

There was a quality of control about the word 'expression' which did not describe adequately what was happening when David and many of the other children were trying to get out and get rid of some of their more intolerable feelings and ideas. A word was sought which would encompass the more constructive forms of expression as well as such behaviours as swearing, spitting, making messes, emitting cries of anguish, and walking on tables – a quite popular and common pursuit in times of acute distress.

'Externalisation', as it is defined by Jack Novick and Anne Hurry in their paper 'Projection and Externalisation', came close to what was required. They refer to it as a general and helpful term under which could be subsumed 'all those processes which lead to the *subjective allocation of inner phenomena to the outer world'* (Novick and Hurry, 1969, p. 8).

Daunted by the complexities and controversies surrounding such concepts as projection and externalisation, and after a prolonged consideration of them, it was decided, as with the term 'the unpleasurable', to throw in the theoretical towel and merely choose the word which most closely depicted what the children were doing. That word was 'externalising'.

Two main kinds of externalising were identified. The less controlled kind in many ways resembled in tone Margaret Mahler's description of the infant's effort to achieve homeostasis. She speaks of such tension-reducing attempts as 'urinating, defecating, coughing, sneezing, spitting, regurgitating, vomiting, all the ways by which the infant tries to rid himself of unpleasurable tension' (Mahler, 1969, p. 8). She also comments that one effect of these 'expulsive phenomena' is to gain the gratification of the 'mother's ministrations' (ibid.). This was compatible with the opinion that, when they were out of control or in overt distress, the children were, however inappropriately, merely demonstrating that they would need help in their attempt to resolve some of their difficulties. All forms of externalising, even the most extreme, were perceived on one level as a prelude to, or a preliminary part of, that attempt.

47

The other kind of externalising was almost entirely purposeful in quality and intention. It was evident in all those interactions with the materials or with the worker in which the child was making a comparatively controlled effort to attend to its concerns, in whatever form, on the 'outside'.

There had been no indications at any time that merely offloading unresolved experience had any beneficial effect other than reducing tension and producing a temporary relief. It was therefore considered important, whenever possible, to incline the children towards the more constructive forms of externalising and expression.

The importance of the materials to assist in this task cannot be overestimated. They functioned, in conjunction with the worker, like a bridge between the two forms of externalising. This had been discovered with David, when they were observed to be a very effective means of helping him to deal with even some of his more extravagant moods.

They can incline the children towards taking responsibility for their own difficulties and help divert them from repetitive and habit-forming behaviours, such as the physical acting-out of distress and the inevitable development of a high level of expectation, as regards an adult intervening to take control of the situation.

Letting the materials take a lot of the strain was the feature of the work which was stressed in later attempts to convince adminis-trators, and others, that an adaptation of the approach being developed in the environment would facilitate its employment by workers from various disciplines in a variety of settings.

13

PROCESS, NOT PLAY

From early on in the enquiry there were two very noticeable features of the children's approach to tray-making. One was the mood of intense preoccupation which they exhibited in the selection, placing and use of the materials within the tray. The other was the clarity with which almost all productions were completed, usually with the comment 'that's it', 'that's me', or 'that's it finished'. Also on completion a sense of calm was noted, as if something had been satisfactorily dealt with or attended to, if only partially or temporarily.

These observations chime with some of those made by Marion Milner in her paper 'The Role of Illusion in Symbol Formation'. Commenting on children playing, she suggests that 'there occurs now and then a particular type of absorption in what they are doing, which gives the impression that something of great importance is going on' (Milner, [1955] 1977, pp. 86–7).

The relationship between tray-making and numerous theories of play was being constantly assessed as the work proceeded, but it was the above observations which first encouraged the idea that the children's involvement with the sand-tray materials was concerned more with process than with play.

The position taken on play was that there should be a quality of enjoyment about it whereas for the majority of the children using the room, their capacity for pleasure was being superseded by their need to attend to what Lawrence Kubie (after Freud) would call 'unfinished business' (Kubie, 1966, p. 194). Some measure of success with this task was thought to be necessary before 'real' play could begin.

This predicament is similar to the one suggested by Freud in relation to the dreams of patients suffering from traumatic neuroses, who are being constantly led back to the situation in which the trauma occurred. In 'Beyond the Pleasure Principle' he wrote: 'We may assume, rather, that dreams are here helping to carry out another task, which must be accomplished before the dominance of the pleasure principle can even begin. These dreams are endeavouring to master the stimulus retrospectively' (Freud, [1920] 1955, p. 32).

An association between dreams and tray-making is made by Louise Eickhoff, a therapist and lecturer in child psychiatry, in her paper entitled 'Dreams in Sand'. Incidentally, she also describes the sand-tray materials as 'the most therapeutically exciting and satisfying medium in my experience' (Eickhoff, 1952, p. 235).

If the connection she makes is accepted, it supports the proposition that, for children attempting to deal symbolically with traumas and their effects, the sand tray provides them with the opportunity to do so while they are awake.

14

THREE RELUCTANCES

In direct conflict with the children's need to externalise the unpleasurable aspects of their experience was the often equally vehement need not to do so. This reluctance to reveal could be equated on a general level with the anthropological opinion of J. van Baal who, in *Symbols for Communication,* suggests that: 'At the bottom of one's heart there is a deep need for concealment counteracting the need for expression; the self must be protected' (van Baal, [1971] 1985, p. 155).

Whilst accepting this as a likely underlying element within the children's total response to the environment, other processes were obviously indicated in this need to withhold. It was assumed, for example, in a room in which there is an implicit request for expression in one form or another, that if it had been accessible to the ear the deep rumbling of repressed material, resisting being brought to conscious awareness, would have been continually heard.

It became obvious that any comprehensive discussion of these and related issues would require further extensive study and would be well beyond the scope of this account. But three reluctances were identified which were considered capable of providing a starting point from which to develop a fuller understanding of the subject.

It had already been discerned that a substantial contribution to that understanding would be found in the work of W. R. D. Fairbairn. His paper 'The Repression and the Return of Bad Objects (with special reference to the "War Neuroses")' (1943) was to become a major influence on the outcome of the whole enquiry.

The first of the three reluctances was observed in the work with a girl aged ten who had been tormented at times by the conflict between her need to be rid of remembered bad experiences and her fear of revealing them. Something of its nature can best be illustrated by a description of how it manifested itself, in a practical sense, in some of the early and quite typical responses she had to the environment, and through a brief account of some of the background experiences which influenced them.

Visits to the environment frequently began with her standing at the door shouting abuse and throwing almost any objects within reach across the room, usually in the direction of the worker. Once inside the room she had a propensity for making messes. Paint had a spectacularly strong appeal. When she eventually reached the big desk, the place she both wanted to be but was terrified of, she would use scores of sheets of newsprint on which to frantically draw pictures and scribble swear-words and secret messages. Within these were 'hidden' many of the issues which most concerned her. She would then cut, tear and sometimes staple bits of them together.

This very active kind of visit alternated with others in which she would enter the room quietly and begin making a tray, often moving on from there to another activity and then over to the big desk. On these more composed occasions, it was as if she wanted to familiarise herself with the desk, in preparation for using it another time.

Again, as had been observed with David and other children, the gradual reduction in the more outrageous forms of expression coincided with an increase in her ability to talk about the feelings and the experiences which she perceived as bad. The time at the door got shorter and the time at the big desk grew longer.

In the story which she eventually told she had, as far back as she could remember, been stealing food and then money and then both. Her time at school had been particularly miserable. Two of her most awful memories were of defecating in the school corridor after being put out of class and of stealing money from her teacher's purse and replacing it with stones. It was in this same teacher's class, where she had been kept for three consecutive years, that she had been persistently and publicly informed that she had the devil in her.

At the age of eight she was admitted as an in-patient to a department of child psychiatry in a local hospital. No one, as far as she could remember, ever explained why and during much of her time there she had experienced intense feelings of grief, associated with the deaths of three members of her extended family. An uncle, for whom she had had a specially strong and long-held affection, had died in distressing circumstances in a fire.

One of her major anxieties was the fear of being mad. This had intensified shortly before her arrival at the unit when, on one of several occasions during which she had completely lost control, she had smashed up a therapy room.

It took over a year, using her own measure of 5 per cent at a time, to reach what she insisted was a 100 per cent disclosure of all she knew and felt to have been troubling her. She was, she said, greatly relieved. And she appeared to be so.

There had been, of course, deeper levels of interaction between us than those indicated here. Whether or not the serious underlying difficulties, relating to her mother's severe post-natal depression and the very haphazard feeding she had received as a baby, had been alleviated in any radical sense, can only be surmised. On a return visit to the unit, a year after moving on to secondary school, she provided her own explanation for her particular reluctance to reveal. She stated simply that she had been frightened of being seen, or thought of, as bad.

The same kind of reluctance, manifesting itself in similar ways, was observed in the responses of many of the other children who used the room. It was particularly evident in the behaviour of those who had been sexually abused. If this had also been one of her concerns, it had never made any overt symbolic or graphic appearance, and when it had been aired as a possible factor in her distress she had refuted it easily.

The issue of sexual abuse surfaced remarkably often as the environment developed.

The second reluctance, although similar in most respects, had one essentially different characteristic. It involved, in substantial measure, an externally imposed restriction on the child, mainly through enticements or threats, not to reveal certain information to another person.

Another significant feature of the reluctance, and the one to be focused on here, was the often quite marked and visible change in the child's emotional and, in some circumstances, physiological disposition, once it had been overcome. This change had been especially noticeable with a boy who, for some of the reasons given above but mainly out of loyalty and fear of rejection by his mother, had accepted with great discomfort to himself her imposed restriction that he must never speak to anyone about what was happening at home. Some of the information he was expected to contain concerned incidents in which he had been allowed, and possibly encouraged, to watch acts of sexual intercourse taking place between older members of the family and visiting adults.

Some features of his behaviour and general appearance were particularly conspicuous. Any altercation involving himself, or taking place between other people in his vicinity, would immediately unbalance an already precarious equilibrium and plunge him into a display of writhing body movements. These were often accompanied by sounds reminiscent of an animal in pain. He frequently looked flushed and his hands and body were almost always damp with sweat.

There were apparently no medical reasons for these symptoms. Information that he had been diagnosed as having a mild form of epilepsy before coming to the unit was checked out, but not confirmed. There was also evidence that his mother sometimes administered a liquid tranquilliser 'to calm him down'. It was realised later, when he felt free to talk, that an added complication was the serious difficulty he had in finding the words to describe his experiences. This proved to be an issue for many of the children and is one which would be worth investigating at some future time.

This child's imposed silence had been kept for years but, mainly as a consequence of the pressure being exerted by other workers involved in the case, his mother was persuaded of the child's need to talk about what was troubling him. She reluctantly withdrew the restrictions and gave him permission to do so. Over the next few days, this resulted in a steady disclosure of a whole series of profoundly distressing events and incidents. It was made mostly to his class teacher, with my assistance. He became almost immediately paler, drier and calmer, and remained like this until a few weeks later when his mother, for a variety of reasons, some of which were legal, replaced the restrictions. The 'symptoms' just as clearly returned.

There were sufficient indications of the reduction and disappearance of minor ailments and discomforts, as a result of the purposeful expression of certain of the children's difficulties, to suggest that some kind of formal study of the issue, involving a medical component, should be considered.

The feature of the reluctances which became the major focus of interest was the high level of acute distress which inevitably accompanied them. It had been observed that the degree of distress accompanying the reluctance was not always commensurate with the perceived severity of the experience about to be revealed. For example, the same intensity of distress was being exhibited in relation to such apparently disparate events as a boy breaking his bicycle, a mother having a bruised cheekbone and a girl being sexually abused by her father.

It had also been observed that this distress reached a peak at the moment when the desire to give verbal expression to a bad experience was about to overcome the fears which were associated with its prospective release. At this point of almost no return the unresolved bad experience seemed to be pushing for release in such a way that the child, experiencing it as unbearable, was having extreme difficulty in continuing to manage it internally, while the anticipated consequences of its release were also unbearable.

This was a 'state of mind' which could subside and recur over a prolonged period of time until, as far as the child was concerned, the worker and the environment were felt to be providing the 'right' conditions for its release.

It was to these fears and anticipations, which were associated with the release of the bad experience, that the amount of distress being produced was believed to most directly relate. It will not be pursued further in this context although it is recognised to be one of several major issues which would require extensive clarification before a thorough understanding of these reluctances could be achieved.

The third reluctance was perceived mainly as a reluctance to let go. Its existence had been indicated first in the sand-tray constructions of a boy who, over a six-month period, took a group of monsters and 'baddies' through a series of intense escapades and events.

Amongst various activities during that time they fled, hid, slept, got away, laughed at themselves, woke up, went underground, got trapped and bounced harmlessly until eventually, and reluctantly, in a very protracted process, they were finally killed off. They were then brought back as wax models before being carefully got rid of again. Their final demise was timed to occur several days before the boy moved on to a residential school. The significance of this timing is not fully understood, although the sense that he had thoroughly finished with the monsters was palpable. I suspect that he had given up on them sometime before this but, becoming aware of my poorly-disguised interest in their demise, had prolonged the final act until it suited him.

On a return visit two months after leaving, he made a tray in which the monsters had reappeared. He accompanied the production with several comments, including: 'The monsters have returned but they're just mirages, but the police are still shooting at them, and the police ape's diving at them but they're just ghosts because they're all dead, they were dead long ago, you saw them go didn't you?'

It was this boy's 'fondness' for these elements and his apparent reluctance to let go, or to give up on them, which had first brought the children's work and the ideas of Ronald Fairbairn into sponta- neous association. There was a specific catalyst for this coming

together: it was the word 'devotion', and it had jumped out of the
following paragraph:

> The actual overcoming of repression as such would, accordingly, appear
> to constitute if anything a less formidable part of the analyst's difficult
> task than the overcoming of the patient's devotion to his repressed objects
> – a devotion which is all the more difficult to overcome because these
> objects are bad and he is afraid of their release from the unconscious.
> (Fairbairn, [1943] 1952, p. 73)

The significance of this 'association', and the possible connections
between the devoted bad object and 'fond' symbolic elements, are
only beginning to be considered. Meanwhile everything which was
being said, done, or produced in the room was appraised with these
factors in mind. Early concerns that the presence of this kind of
reluctance, permeating the children's responses, might require that
substantial modifications be made to the approach which was being
developed, were soon dispelled. It seemed that whether it was fear
or 'fondness' which was fuelling the children's reluctance to reveal,
or to let go of the bad experience, their need to experience the worker
and the environment as good remained the same.

Fairbairn's paper on the repression of bad objects was introduced
at the beginning of the section; further words from it provide a
decidedly pertinent if seemingly oblique conclusion. Their relevance
will hopefully become more apparent later.

> The moral would seem to be that the appeal of a good object is an indis-
> pensable factor in promoting a dissolution of the cathexis of internalised
> bad objects. (Fairbairn, [1943] 1952, p. 74)

15

A Remarkable Container

There was an increasing sense of cohesiveness and structure about the environment as the activities became more defined and as various rituals and limits were consolidated. Based on the continuing abundance of unpleasurable experience finding expression, it seemed as if the conditions necessary to assist the externalising process and to overcome certain reluctances had, in some measure, been achieved.

In appraising which of the many features and influences within the room were contributing to these conditions, the sand tray's capacity to contain aspects of unresolved experience in symbolic form appeared to be a major factor. The role of the sand tray as a container was one of three basic attributes which were now beginning to be appreciated as indispensable to the approach being developed.

The others were its potential as a symbolic medium of expression, which has already been indicated in the various references to the children's symbolic work, and its ability to initiate and sustain creative activity. Both will be commented on more extensively later.

Any appreciation of the sand tray's potential as a container is dependent, to some degree, on accepting the premise that small toys and objects can function as symbolic vehicles or, as contended here, receptacles, for certain constituents and components of the children's experience. In a description reminiscent of the nursery rhyme 'The House that Jack Built', it could be said that here are the toys which contain the experience, here is the sand which contains the toys, here is the frame which contains the sand, and here is the tray which contains it all.

The perceived importance of the frame of the sand tray and of the frame provided by the edges of the paper in Talk and Draw, prompted a long search for writers commenting on the subject. It began and ended with Marion Milner, who remarks: 'The frame marks off the different kind of reality that is within it from that which is outside it' (Milner, [1955] 1977, p. 86).

For the present, until a better understanding is attained, the frame is seen simply as a means of circumscribing an area, onto or into which, aspects of experience can be safely externalised and con-

57

templated symbolically, without their getting too scattered or falling over the edges. Of possible significance are words by D. W. Winnicott about the infant who has had no one person 'to gather his bits together' (Winnicott, [1945] 1982, p. 150). On first reading, this phrase had activated an image of a sand tray with a well-defined frame, providing a child with the opportunity to symbolically and retrospectively get to work on the task.

The sand tray's capacity to contain seemed to be substantially reinforced by two associated procedures. In one of these, the various stories and comments which usually accompanied the children's tray constructions were very carefully received and recorded in writing. In the other, through the photographing of the constructions, it became possible for an unpleasurable issue to be taken into the camera, held on film, processed and then returned to the child at a later date, in a more acceptable form, as a nice picture. This would of course be applicable to anything which the children produced and which was then photographed.

There is a rather loose equation here between the process taking place through the camera and the modification of infantile fears which, as Wilfred Bion suggests in reference to ideas by Melanie Klein, occurs during their 'sojourn in the good breast' (Bion, [1962] 1988, p. 90). In *Learning from Experience*, he wrote: 'they are felt to have been modified in such a way that the object that is re-introjected has become tolerable to the infant's psyche' (ibid.).

The quality of the worker in this interaction is not underestimated; what effect the quality of the camera or the photograph might have on the process is open to speculation.

Even from the earliest days of presenting the sand tray to children, when it had been used in isolation from other creative materials, it had been suspected of being a remarkable container. And, from the moment it had been introduced into the room, part of its attraction for the children seemed to be as an alternative receptacle, however temporary, for some of the intolerable concerns which many of them had been hauling around for years, with little prospect of relief.

Now, in its developing role as core container within the environment, its effectiveness was seen to be both dependent on, and increased by, all the other materials and procedures which supported and surrounded it, extending outwards to include the walls, the floor and the ceiling.

Whilst everything in the room eventually amalgamated to create a containing entity, at the centre of it all was the sand tray, functioning in close and complementary association with two other main containers. These were the worker and the activity of Talk and Draw, both of which were particularly impressive in their capacity to receive and absorb distress! Together these three containers seemed capable of conveying to the children the profoundly reassuring message that, whatever they needed to bring to the room and whatever its intensity, it could be unequivocally held.

An adequate consideration of the value and importance of Talk and Draw would require a separate presentation. Its supreme characteristic, perhaps, was that nearly all the children had an immediate and positive response to it. Those who did not were easily and pleasurably introduced through a version of D. W. Winnicott's 'Squiggle Game', which is extensively described and documented in his book *Therapeutic Consultations in Child Psychiatry* (Winnicott, 1971).

It was the capacity of the environment as a whole to contain all that was brought to it which was eventually acknowledged as the fundamental requirement for creating the conditions for safe externalising. The same conditions were soon recognised to be just as important in establishing the kind of space and atmosphere in which the children's ideas and experience could be fully and creatively explored. And it was this creative activity which now began to gain acceptance as a prerequisite for any therapeutic change in how the children were functioning.

16

THE CREATIVE SPACE

The kind of space which evolved had qualities in common with most other environments, both educational and therapeutic, which are devised as places where children can safely create and play. For example it resembled, in various respects, what Estelle Weinrib (referring to the ideas of the sandplay therapist Dora Kalff[7]) describes as 'the free and protected space'; 'the necessary security space'; a place where there is 'no confrontation, no intellectualization or interpretation', and where 'the therapist knows consciously what the patient knows unconsciously' (Weinrib, 1983, pp. 27–9).

It also fulfilled at least two of J. L. Singer's 'Conditions Conducive to Image-Formation' and the 'Set to Reprocessing in Children', by providing 'An opportunity for privacy and for practice in a relatively protected setting where the external environment is reasonably redundant so that greater attention can be focused on internal activity' (Singer, 1975, p. 198). And, not to be underestimated, an 'Availability of a variety of materials' (ibid.).

Of the many other comparisons which were explored, the affinities of most significance were located in the concept of 'the potential space', or, as it is alternatively defined by D. W. Winnicott in 'The Location of Cultural Experience', the *'third area'* (Winnicott, 1966, pp. 371, 372).

The resemblances between the environment as it had evolved and the potential space are suggested in the following comments taken from the same paper. As will be apparent in the section entitled 'Going Back with Bobos', the fact that they refer to the experience of a baby only enhances their applicability.

> The potential space only happens *in relation to a feeling of confidence* on the part of the baby, that is, confidence related to the dependability of the mother-figure or environmental elements. (Winnicott, 1966, p. 371)

> Every baby has his or her own favourable or unfavourable experience here. (Ibid.)

---

[7] Her book, entitled *Sandplay*, is included in the list of references.

In favourable circumstances the potential space becomes filled with the products of the baby's own creative imagination. (Ibid.)

It can be looked upon as sacred to the individual in that it is here that the individual experiences creative living. (Ibid., p. 372)

There were several similarities between the two 'spaces', and the references to 'creative imagination' and 'creative living' were of particular interest. They fitted well with the increasingly robust stance being taken on the importance of creative activity to the children's therapeutic task. There were two ways in which it was perceived as influential. Firstly, as already indicated, it was felt that creative flow and expression could play a very active part in helping to overcome reluctances and assist in the externalising of the unpleasurable.

The quality of this kind of creative activity is similar to that which Herbert Read, in *Education Through Art,* describes as 'Free or spontaneous expression.' He defines it as the 'unconstrained exteriorization of the mental activities of thinking, feeling, sensation and intuition' (Read, 1943, p. 112).

Spontaneity, as it was observed in the work with the children, seemed to act as a catalyst on the psyche, supplying that extra momentum which can be useful in bringing about the effective release of a bad experience which has resisted all previous appeals. Herbert Read also notes, in the same volume, its value in a more general sense: 'the secret of our collective ills is to be traced to the suppression of spontaneous creative ability in the individual' (ibid., p. 202).

The unpleasurable and the unfavourable products of the children's creative imagination were viewed as descriptive variations of the same phenomenon; whatever the name, there was now little doubt that the environment was getting filled up with them. It was in relation to what happens once they have been put out there that creative activity – functioning as an agent of change – was believed to be playing its other most important and vital role.

Lawrence Kubie discusses this ability to effect change, and also how it can be restricted, in his paper 'Impairment of the Freedom to Change with the Acquisition of the Symbolic Process.' The 'prison wardens', to which he refers in the following quotation, are identified by him as the rigidity of conscious processes at one end, and the rigidity of unconscious functions at the other. If not totally overcome by the pressures of creative flow and activity, these wardens were certainly frequently stunned by them. Kubie writes:

The uniqueness of creativity – its capacity to sort out bits of experience
and put them together into new combinations – depends on the extent
to which preconscious functions can operate freely between these two
ubiquitous concurrent and oppressive prison wardens. (Kubie, 1974,
p. 259)

His comments, which have obvious implications as regards reluctances and the release of the bad experience, also seem to affirm the
idea that it is only when there has been some degree of success in
externalising the unpleasurable that the creative or re-creative work
can begin. Although it was assumed that the children's purposes were
being played out throughout the whole environment and that each
activity had an essential contribution to make, the sand tray was
found to be the foremost medium of creative expression. It was
capable not only of illustrating and demonstrating the children's
creative intentions, but also helping to fulfil them. The creative
activity taking place in the sand tray seemed to be mainly concerned
with an exploration of the symbolic elements of the children's
experience, and was intended to bring about some change or transformation in them.

Something of the practical nature of the task in which the children
were involved, although referring to objects other than those being
considered here, is indicated by Jean Piaget: 'in order to know
objects, the subject must act upon them, and therefore transform
them: he must displace, connect, combine, take apart, and re-
assemble them' (Piaget, 1970, p. 704).

The sand tray's capacity to facilitate creative expression is perhaps
worth stressing. Because the procedure of tray-making requires no
skill, it provides an immediate and almost effortless opportunity for
creative expression for anyone capable of selecting an object and
placing it in the sand. Also, depending on an adequate supply of
toys and materials, an infinite number of combinations and constructions can be produced, from simple to highly complex.
Profound changes can be easily and swiftly effected, as the inclusion
or extraction of even one object could negatively or positively alter
the meaning of an entire production.

If one accepts that the environment had evolved in direct response
to the children's needs and requests, then it could be argued that,
consciously or otherwise, they had produced the kind of space in
which to attempt some of the creative living which, for most of
them, had been decidedly unsatisfactory first time round.

In D. W. Winnicott's scenario, 'the potential space' becomes filled with the favourable and unfavourable products of the children's creative imagination. As far as this environment was concerned there had been, at least in the early stages of each child's experience of it, a preponderance of the unfavourable kind. The remedy for this imbalance was thought to lie in the provision of good and new experiences. Not only were they necessary to make life more pleasant in the short term, but they would provide the raw materials out of which would be derived the positive symbolic elements considered essential for the children's creative and remedial endeavours to proceed. Their effectiveness in this respect would be dependent on their quality and the circumstances in which they were provided.

In a symposium on the creative process in science and medicine, Manfred Eigen comments on new interpretations in molecular biology and the benefits of putting new experiences with old knowledge. He suggests that: 'You cannot be creative until you have new experiences. So is not creation mainly a rearranging of all our experiences, making new combinations among them?' (Krebs and Shelley, 1975, p. 10). In the light of the unchanging themes and features which were frequently observed in the children's symbolic constructions, and which appeared to involve an interminable working-over of the same symbolic elements, producing rearrangements of the same unsatisfactory formulations, the need to bring new elements in contact with old, to facilitate creative change, seemed a very reasonable proposition.

With this issue uppermost in mind, the children's attention now seemed to turn toward what has been defined as their need for nourishment.

17

GOING BACK WITH BOBOS

About the same time as the conditions for safe externalising were becoming well established, what I perceived as an increased request for intake and nourishment was first recognised and thought to be heralded by a developing demand for 'bobos'. One boy had said that when he was a baby he had called his feeding bottle a 'bobo', and subsequently everyone who came to the room used this word.

Previous to this 'demand', a toy feeding-bottle, which was later replaced by a real one when its top was chewed off, had been used almost entirely for the feeding of inanimate objects. King Kong and a cracked stone were among the main beneficiaries. Once one of the children had taken some milk from the real bottle, others swiftly joined in and very soon 'having a bobo' was accepted as just another available activity within the room.

At the height of their popularity, which once reached never wavered, the demand for bobos was such that it became necessary to have a clean sterilised bottle available for each child, every day. They were usually filled with school milk, or milk which I brought in each morning, and sometimes, when there was a preference for it, with water.

Cups were also available to allow for a choice of drinking container and for children who were very thirsty. A boy who was known to have been very well-fed and tended to as a baby was the only child to be comfortably uninterested in using a bottle; he took an occasional drink of milk from a cup.

Although there were many occasions when children were intensely involved in having a bobo, their use of them rarely seemed to produce what might be termed overt regressive behaviours. A favourite place for having one, as indicated earlier, was the large wooden box on wheels. But, overall, bobos were most frequently taken as an accompaniment to a chosen creative activity.

The word nourishment, as it is being used here, is meant to imply any kind of good or satisfactory experience which a child, if able or inclined to, could pleasurably internalise. It was assumed that the children's need for nourishment was being met in several main ways: within the room it involved anything from a straightforward feed using crisps, apples or milk, to one in which the same food was being

64

used, but which, because of the quality of the interaction (between the one who was feeding and the one who was being fed), a nourishment of a more intangible but significant nature was believed to be occurring.

The children's main source of nourishment was thought to be through their relationships and in particular those with the worker and their class teacher. The development of a combined approach to the child, involving these two relationships, became an important feature of the work and provided, when effective, what came to be referred to as parallel or double nourishment. The circumstances in which a child could have a special person throughout the day (and for as many days or months as required) to regress and work up through the relationship were no longer available in the unit. They had been known in past times.

The other main source of nourishment was everything of a positive kind which was being supplied by the unit as a whole. Ideally this would consist of a well-structured and enriching educational resource, set up in such a way that its demands and encouragements would be geared to the children's capacity to make genuine use of them as their dominant concerns began to find some resolution.

Whether or not there was any direct relationship, on a general level between the establishment of a safe place to externalise and the increased request for intake, a connection between the two events had certainly been indicated on an individual level, in the work with David.

As suggested earlier, it was only after he had externalised and partially resolved his most acute bad experiences that he was able to take in information and receive and utilise what was available to him within the room, and later within the unit. This had been particularly evident in his relationship with me.

It had also been noted with David and others that, given sufficient time and opportunity to indulge in either of the two processes of externalising or internalising, a natural and changing balance between them was achieved. The child's inner need, or readiness, to be attending to one process or the other has obvious and important implications for all aspects of work with children.

The benefits of bobos were believed to be twofold: first, on a general level, they were just one of several features of the environment which contributed to its being the kind of space in which the children would feel at ease to pursue their therapeutic purposes; second, on a more specific level, they were viewed as a means of facilitating the child's return to developmentally earlier times, to catch up on lost, missed-out, or previously unsatisfactory feeding experiences. And more than this, as implied earlier, if the return was taking place in 'favourable circumstances' then more than milk would be internalised, and more than the feed would be re-experienced.

Of the many situations in which children seemed to be making a direct trip backwards, one which left a particularly clear impression concerned a girl who had taken over a year to reveal slowly a series of traumatic incidents. These were mainly associated with having been sexually abused by a neighbour, and with the loss and death of several dogs to whom she had been very attached. Settling down with a bobo in the big wooden box and covering herself with the blanket one relaxed day, she talked spontaneously about how she had persistently refused to use a bottle as a baby and how her mother had resorted to dipping her dummy in milk, in an attempt to get her to feed. She smiled at the prospect of what her mother would say if she could see her there with the bobo. She said she would be telling her about how she liked them now when she got home.

The possible benefits of a return to earlier times are suggested by Bruno Bettelheim in his paper 'Regression as Progress': 'It is a recapturing of early experience through a partial re-experience that will support a very different development' (Bettelheim, 1972, p. 191). Another kind of going back is indicated by E. H. Erikson who, in writing about play procedures similar to tray-making, proposes that they 'may well facilitate in a child an impulse to recapitulate and, as it were, to re-invent his own experience' (Erikson, 1972, p. 132).

Whatever the exact processes envisaged by these two writers to be involved in these 'returns to earlier times', both statements were in accord with the ideas being formulated to explain what was happening on a symbolic level, throughout the children's work, and in particular in their use of the sand tray. As far as I was concerned, in both the direct form of going back with a bobo, and the more oblique one through the use of the sand tray, a symbolic process was involved.

It was the ideas of Susanne Langer which provoked the leap into the premise that all good and new experiences would be the source for the new symbolic elements necessary for the children's re-creative and reconstructive work. From my first encounter with her ideas in *Philosophy in a New Key* (Langer, [1942] 1957) there had been an immediate recognition of the affinity between her theoretical contentions and the children's symbolic practice.

Those ideas have pervaded many of the comments on the children's symbolic activity which have been made so far and, as will be seen later, were important in understanding what kind of symbolic processes were manifesting themselves in the children's work. It was two interrelated references from the book which had been directly responsible for my conjecturings on symbolic elements. These were:

> The material furnished by the senses is constantly wrought into *symbols*, which are our elementary ideas. Some of these ideas can be combined and manipulated in the manner we call 'reasoning.' (Langer, [1942] 1957, p. 42)

And in a similar statement with a different emphasis:

> For if the material of thought is symbolism, then the thinking organism must be forever furnishing symbolic versions of its experiences, in order to let thinking proceed. (Ibid., p. 41)

If one accepts that the children were involved in furnishing symbolic versions of the good and new experiences available to them, and that out of these would be derived the necessary symbolic elements for their re-creative and reconstructive work, then the increased demand for nourishment would make very reasonable sense. As a consequence, there is only slight hesitation in suggesting that the children's demand for bobos had been generated by their own instinctive understanding of what they needed.

By this stage of the enquiry there had been a sufficient number of trays demonstrating a reduction in the unpleasurable themes and features, and an increase in the nourishing and reconstructive ones, to encourage the idea that something positive may have been happening for some of the children. Unfortunately, there had also been enough examples of constructions in which the negative elements remained totally unchanged to suggest that, whatever the environment was providing, for some children it was not enough.

This lack of change was viewed as the consequence of the environment's failure to meet the children's needs in several ways. The worker and the environment were not being experienced as safe enough, or good enough, to risk revealing or letting go of the bad experience. They were also failing to provide enough nourishment at a deep enough level to have a radical effect on past difficulties, or to counteract the negative influences experienced by the children in their lives outside the unit.

The prolonged persistence of these negative features was taken as a sign that only with a different worker or in a different setting, and possibly a residential one, would there be any hope of loosening the log jam. The acceptance that the child's life and relationships outside the unit often overwhelmed any attempts to work constructively within the environment did not detract from the attempt to assess what might be achieved there.

Needless to say, going back with a bobo and the worker was considered to be the most effective way of providing the children with the nourishment they needed at the depth it was required. As far as the children's reconstructive intentions were concerned, it might be said that the deeper the nourishment the better the bricks.

Going back with the sand tray was perceived of as an entirely different procedure, in which a symbolic return was being made to the old symbolised elements of previous experiences. In the arena of the sand tray, the purpose was to reconsider and work on them, alongside any new symbolic elements, in an attempt to bring about their transformation.

The possibility of bringing the symbolised elements of one's entire existence into proximity is advocated by Lawrence Kubie, among others, in 'Psychoanalysis and Scientific Method'. Commenting on the symbolic process, as he perceives it, and employing a revised statement from an earlier paper (Kubie, 1957), he cites this as one of its several essential functions:

> ... whereas on conscious levels, and to an uncertain degree on precon-
> scious levels, we can sharply distinguish the past from the present, and
> the near from the far, on the more obscure levels of dynamic unconscious
> processes, near and far, past, present, and future all fuse into a continuum
> so complete that differentiation among them is lost. (Kubie, 1959, p. 74)

How lost they become is arguable.

David Beres, in his paper 'Symbol and Object', proposes a similar propensity:

> Only with the capacity to form mental representations and to express
> them in symbols is the human being able to relate the present to the past
> and to the future, to evoke the absent object, and to recall as well as to
> remember. (Beres, 1965, p. 19)

Being able to bring together all the various symbolic elements of experience, past, present and anticipated, in the external arena of the sand tray, is central to the therapeutic aspirations of this paper.

18

Aspects of Symbolic Activity

Following on from the suggestions that all the various positive and negative elements of the children's experience could be represented and brought together in the external arena of the sand tray, attention was turned more firmly to a consideration of what exactly was happening to them once they were out there.

Ideas on the issue are still in the process of being clarified but it seemed likely that several different aspects of symbolic activity could be involved in what the children were doing. They seemed to extend from a kind of symbolic thinking or processing, through a symbolic reprocessing to a symbolic reconstruction.

In symbolic thinking, the children were assumed to be mainly concerned with a relatively superficial exploration and working-over of recent ideas, information and experience in a continual pursuit of understanding and satisfactory assimilation. This process was also viewed as a means of keeping issues 'loose', thereby preventing the laying down or creation of new, distorted features or the build-up and further consolidation of previously unresolved ones. There will be more about this in the following section.

It was felt that this level of symbolic activity could proceed successfully without any input or assistance from the worker. In contrast, symbolic reconstruction, at its most basic level, would require the worker to be extensively involved both directly and indirectly. Symbolic reprocessing was thought to lie somewhere between the two, both in relation to the depth at which it occurred and to the degree to which the worker would need to be involved.

There is a possible parallel between the kind of symbolic thinking which is being proposed here, and that which is described by Jacques Monod in the symposium on the creative process mentioned earlier. The toys and objects in a tray are being equated with the circles and the squares on the blackboard.

... when a scientist is interested in a given phenomenal situation, what he does, perhaps without realising it, is to try to simulate the situation subjectively to achieve a form of internal representation, first of the phenomenon itself and the sources involved and so on. I have discussed

69

this with physicists, including highly abstract theoretical physicists, and they have told me that in thinking about a phenomenon that they are interested in, they more or less identify themselves with an electron or a particle and ask, what would I do if I were that particle. This process of simulation may become verbal but need not be so and indeed, in fact, begins by non-verbal representations. (Krebs and Shelley, 1975, p. 4)

He continues:

... we had taken the custom of symbolising this assumption by writing, for instance, circles for one conformation and squares for the other. This symbolism became somewhat more complicated when we began writing events occurring in an enzyme involving several subunits. A possible interpretation of these systems occurred to me, in fact, when standing in front of a blackboard using such symbolism in an attempt to find a description of actual experimental data. (Ibid., p. 5)

There appeared to be similarities also between the thinking on the outside, which was taking place in the arena of the sand tray, and the thinking on the inside as a prelude or a rehearsal for action, as described here by Freud in 'Anxiety and Instinctual Life':

Thinking is an experimental action carried out with small amounts of energy, in the same way as a general shifts small figures about on a map before setting his large bodies of troops in motion. (Freud, [1933] 1964, p. 89)

In symbolic reprocessing it seemed likely that elements of previously unresolved experience were being reappraised in conditions more conducive to their resolution, and in the light of an increased maturity. Such experiences would come close, in kind and quality, to what J. L. Singer, in *Daydreaming and Fantasy*, describes as 'faulty assimilations' (Singer, 1975, p. 184), and which he proposes can be 'relatively quickly resolved, in the sense that the child tries them out and is corrected by adults or by circumstances'. He goes on to say: 'But many are not tried out directly because of lack of opportunity, or the child's shame at expressing private notions, or simply because the material is not appropriate for direct communication until later in life' (ibid.).

The possibility of a retrospective resolution can also be read into Freud's statement that 'it is not to be wondered at if the ego, so long as it is feeble, immature and incapable of resistance, fails to deal with tasks which it could cope with later on with the utmost ease' (Freud, [1940] 1964, pp. 184–5).

Based on the children's response to the sand-tray materials in the environment, and the experience of them in other settings, there had been a growing conviction that these lighter levels of symbolic activity could be practised in any relatively secure setting with only the minimum involvement of an adult. This, of course, would make them a potentially superb resource for young children in most educational environments. This notion is supported by E. H. Erikson who, in a continuation of his remarks on the child's impulse to reinvent its experience writes, 'we may entertain the dim hope that some such play procedure may become an adjunct to early education rather than remain a method in the service of the clinic or of research only' (Erikson, 1972, p. 132).

Symbolic reconstruction was thought to be similar in many respects to symbolic reprocessing in its preoccupation with some sort of retrospective remedy for previously unresolved experience. In this case, however, the changes and transformations being sought would be concerned with the deeper levels of the children's experience, touching, if the conditions were right, on the earliest and most damaged areas of it. Something of its perceived purpose and function is suggested in this comment by Harry Guntrip:

> ... the deepest researches of contemporary psychoanalysis show that 'radical' psychotherapy must aim, not simply at the resolution of specific conflicts, but at the fundamental regrowing of the basic ego, the whole personal self (with the proviso that such 'radical' psychotherapy is certainly not possible or even wanted in every case ... (Guntrip, [1952] 1968, p. 317)

This whole endeavour had stemmed mainly from a sense of disillusionment that the majority of the children who had been attending the unit for years had remained untouched at a deep enough level to effect any real change in how they were able to deal with themselves and the rest of the world. It was only once the environment had become well established that the depth of response required by some of the children began to be apparent.

Something of what was needed had been understood in the work with David, but the first time it was fully appreciated was with a boy who will be introduced shortly. He was known to have been exposed from birth to recurring intolerable experiences against a background of severe emotional and physical deprivation and his needs became the benchmark for the depth of response which would be required.

If what the environment provided was based on the needs of the children with the most extreme problems, then it would be adequate for those less troubled, allowing them to utilise all that was available when they needed it and to the depth it was required.

In practice, because of circumstances unrelated to the actual working of the environment, it became difficult to sustain this ethos. It was possible, however, to work effectively enough, for long enough, to be convinced that its value to the children would be entirely dependent on the degree to which a symbolic reconstruction could be achieved within it.

The idea of a symbolic reconstruction was acquired in two main ways. It came originally from the work with David, when his attempts to reconstruct the landscape were interpreted as evidence of his constructive intentions and from the perception that what was happening on the 'outside', in the sand tray, was a reflection of what was going on 'inside' the child. And it came from books and papers.

What was conceived in the coming together of these two influences, and why the product was considered to be important to the work, is the subject of the final section.

19

SYMBOLIC RECONSTRUCTION

Throughout the enquiry there had been a continual adopting and discarding of ideas on such issues as symbol formation and function as part of the effort to understand what the children were doing in the sand trays. Those which survived the process and retained their applicability to the practical work are responsible for the speculations which have littered this account so far, and are behind those which will be offered now in bringing it to a conclusion.

Symbol formation and function is an immense and complex subject, and even a comprehensive survey of the study undertaken to get this far – in itself but a drop in the symbolic ocean – would have required a separate presentation.

What follows is a brief selection of some of the most influential of those ideas, interspersed with a few explanatory comments.

The symbolic process thought to be most prevalent in the children's use of the materials is what Susanne Langer defines as non-discursive or presentational symbolism. Something of its nature is conveyed in the following passage from *Philosophy in a New Key*:

> But the symbolism furnished by our purely sensory appreciation of forms is a *non-discursive symbolism*, peculiarly well suited to the expression of ideas that defy linguistic 'projection.' Its primary function, that of conceptualizing the flux of sensations, and giving us concrete *things* in place of kaleidoscopic colours or noises, is itself an office that no language-born thought can replace. (Langer, [1942] 1957, p. 93)

And something of its origins are provided in this one:

> Just as verbal symbolism has a natural evolution from the mere suggestive word or 'word-sentence' of babyhood to the grammatical edifice we call a language, so presentational symbolism has its own characteristic development. It grows from the momentary, single, static image presenting a simple concept, to greater and greater units of successive images having reference to each other; changing scenes, even visions of things in motion. (Ibid., p. 145)

Neither of the terms used by Susanne Langer, nor indeed any of the others encountered elsewhere, were adequate to convey the high image content of the children's activity and until something more apt has been found or devised, it will be referred to as 'non-verbal symbolic activity'.

I had no difficulty with the generally accepted proposition that there are two kinds of symbolic process: the one being focused on here, in which imagery is the predominant component and which is the first, in developmental terms, to make its appearance; and the one which evolves around and out of it, and is concerned mainly with language. Much less appealing was the widely held view that non-verbal symbolic activity becomes, or should become, virtually redundant once language has been well established; and that if it is indulged in with too much enthusiasm afterwards, it implies that there has been a return to developmentally inappropriate levels of functioning, for no worthwhile purpose.

Such ideas, which suggest that a preponderance of non-verbal symbolic activity can delay the acquisition of language, are tenable in relation to the difficulties experienced by individual children, but not in an overall assessment of the process's worth and function. This, of course, is in keeping with having affirmed, in the section on going back with a bobo, the value of a symbolic return to earlier times for the purpose of reconstruction.

In the position eventually reached on the issue, non-verbal symbolic activity is seen as a potentially positive and creative ingredient in the children's functioning which, in the right circumstances, can be utilised by them to assist in the resolution of their concerns.

David Beres was one of the many writers who also took this more positive view. He says, 'symbolism is an ubiquitous process present in all human psychic activity and I do not agree with authors, including Ernest Jones, who state that symbolic activity is a regressive phenomenon' (Beres, 1965, p. 14).

A slightly different but positive perspective is also provided by Emilio Rodrigué in 'Notes on Symbolism'.

> I consider that symbols enable the subject to conceive and elaborate his feelings and ideas concerning his objects. Each representational symbol embodies a conception of it. By means of the multiple symbolic forms a given object can take, the subject can work over and experience all the range of emotions related to his primary objects. (Rodrigué, 1956, p. 157)

Undoubtedly one of the most unexpected outcomes of the enquiry was the discovery, as the profoundly creative nature of the children's symbolic activity began to unfold, that the position taken on this issue was also leading quietly in the direction of C. G. Jung. For example, Robert Moody writing on Jung's concept of the 'living symbol' says: 'It is creative; ... Jung's major point is that symbols are used creatively in dreams, in art, in psychoses and in many social phenomena. Living symbols provide means of active expression leading to the resolution of the present conflict' (Moody, 1956, p. 11).

And if David Beres thinks the symbol is everywhere Robert Moody thinks it is for all time. He continues, 'All psychic development depends upon symbolization; it is symbolic development. This applies to all ages from the cradle to the grave' (ibid., p. 12).

One other Jungian view, on which the case for the positive creative symbol will be temporarily rested, comes from Estelle Weinrib of the 'free protected space'. She states: 'it is a healing agent that acts as a reconciling bridge between opposites' (Weinrib, 1983, p. 23). Then, quoting from Esther Harding's paper 'What Makes The Symbol Effective As A Healing Agent', Weinrib adds that it '"can be regarded as an attempt of the unconscious to lead regressive *libido* into a creative act, thus pointing the way to a resolution of the conflict."' (Ibid.)

Out of the many and diverging opinions on the genesis of symbol formation, the chosen view had been acquired, in part, as a response to ideas on REM sleep in neonates, such as those presented by Paul Miller in his book *Sense and Symbol*. It contends that the symbolisation of experience, consisting of some sort of rudimentary image formation (and a precursor of symbol formation), begins from the moment of birth, if not before, and that through this process the child begins to give shape and meaning to its world.

> REM sleep is present from the moment of birth; in fact, it occupies more time both absolutely and relatively in the neonatal period than in any other time of life. It diminishes from about 50 per cent of sleeping time in the neonate to about 20 per cent in the adult. This does not mean that the neonate dreams in the same fashion as the adult dreams ... .(Miller, 1969, p. 96)

Then, quoting H. Roffwarg *et al.* (1966, p. 611) from a paper entitled 'Ontogenetic Development of the Human Sleep-Dream Cycle', Miller continues:

> 'If by dreaming one means a succession of vivid, discrete yet integrated, hallucinated images, it is hardly likely that newborns, who have

extremely crude patterned vision (Haynes *et al*. 1965), dream.' It does not mean that a total physiological state of REM sleep exists in the neonate similar to that in the child and adult. The infant cannot dream until it has accumulated some images which it can reproduce. (Miller, 1969, pp. 96–7)

The fact that there was so much activity going on was seen as the natural consequence of the child being more intensely involved, than at any other time in its life, in the attempt to deal with an over-whelming input of sensations and experiences. It was assumed therefore, in line with my theoretical bias, that all this activity was commensurate with the laying down of the symbolic foundations of the child's existence.

Another viewpoint which conveys something of the enormous task facing the child in those early days and the circumstances out of which they are attempting to construct an existence, comes from Heinz Werner and Bernard Kaplan in their book on symbol formation.

Thus man, destined to conquer the world through knowing, starts out with confusion, disorientation, and chaos, which he struggles to overcome. This struggle is a never-ceasing process, continuing throughout life: man's objects are always touched with a coefficient of indeterminacy and, as long as he is open to new environments and experiences, they are constantly in the process of transformation, changing in their sig-nificance. One may indeed say that man lives constantly in a world of becoming rather than in a world of being. Now it is our contention that in order to build up a truly human universe, that is, a world that is known rather than merely reacted to, man requires a new tool – an instrumen-tality that is suited for, and enables the realization of, those operations constituting the activity of knowing. This instrumentality is the *symbol*. (Werner and Kaplan, 1963, p. 13)

This accords with my conviction that, providing there is an openness to new environments and experiences, then there is always the pos-sibility of transformation and change. That the symbolisation of experience begins early and continues throughout life, was funda-mental to the therapeutic aspirations of the environment as a whole.

It was mainly through the descriptions of the early days and origins of symbol formation, bringing with them a heightened awareness of the child's vulnerability to the vagaries of its environ-ment – unless exquisite care was being taken by the surrounding adults – that the susceptibility of symbol formation to distortion began to be considered.

Once it had been accepted that the furnishing of symbolic versions of good and nourishing experiences were producing the positive symbolic elements necessary for the children's re-creative and reconstructive work, then it seemed only reasonable, if this argument was being taken to its logical conclusion, to further propose that the symbolisation of traumatic or bad experiences would be likely to produce the negative and the distorted elements.

The effect of trauma on symbol formation was raised earlier in the account. It was conjectured then that those features which had been defined as negative and persistent might be the symbolic representations of internal formulations of a very potent or distorted kind, and that they might be the product of bad or traumatic experiences. These ideas persisted in the face of all subsequent observations. If the child had been exposed to an accumulation of unsatisfactory or acute traumatic experiences during its most tender and vulnerable days, and if these had not been alleviated or counteracted by sufficient good and nourishing ones, then over a prolonged period of time, these early distortions would be added to, consolidated and concretised, to produce an even more grossly distorted symbol formation. It was for these 'distortions', which seemed to be revealing themselves in the most persistent and intractable features of the children's productions, that the environment needed to have a response if it was to be at all effective. That response was what symbolic reconstruction at its most fundamental level was thought to be all about.

Once all the various elements of the children's experience were made available to be explored and worked on within the arena of the sand tray, it was likely that a variety of symbolic recombinations, re-creations and transformations could be taking place. As for the more intractable features and structures, they were felt to be well past being tinkered with. Having been formed by an accumulation of distorted elements and having been slowly and no doubt painfully built up over the years, they were conjectured to have become an integral and embedded aspect of the child's deep internal structures, constantly in need of attention and eliciting a 'fondness' which only intensified their resistance to change and resolution.

As any conversion or modification of them was being ruled out, the only way forward was thought to be through the development of entirely new and separate symbolic structures. These, it was contended, would allow the interest and energy which had been

invested in the old structures to be gradually withdrawn and transferred to the new ones until, very slowly, in the child's own good
time, the old ones would merely crumble and fade away. As in some
ways this process was conceived to be more of a beginning again
than an attempt to change what was there, it could perhaps more
accurately be described as a symbolic *construction*.

This preferred approach to the intractable features can be seen in
the light of W. R. D. Fairbairn's remarks at the end of the section on
the reluctances. Just as he proposed that the 'dissolution of the
cathexis of internalized bad objects' (Fairbairn, [1943] 1952, p. 74)
could be assisted through the appeal of the good object (which in
the context of that discussion would be the analyst), so the giving
up on the old, fond, symbolic structures would be accomplished
through the appeal and attraction of the new and good ones.

In these circumstances, there would be a direct appeal from the
worker through the immediate relationship with the child, and an
indirect one reflecting the extent to which the 'nourishment'
provided by the worker had been satisfactorily internalised and was
being symbolically represented in the new structures.

The success of this symbolic reconstruction is, of course, entirely
dependent on the depth and extent to which the unpleasurable was
being externalised, on the sensitivity of the worker in receiving it,
on the quality and availability of nourishment, and on the depth
to which it was being taken in.

Whilst no claims of any sort will be made as to what kind of
specific internal processes might be involved at these times of
creative construction, there is a quotation from Arthur
Schopenhauer from *The World as Will and Idea*, which evokes the
essence of the experience:

> But ordinarily it is in the obscure depths of the mind that the rumination
> of the materials received from without takes place, through which they
> are worked up into thoughts; and it goes on almost as unconsciously as
> the conversion of nourishment into the humours and substance of the
> body. (Schopenhauer, [1883] 1886, p. 328)

The most direct influence on understanding the susceptibility of
symbol formation to distortion had come from Lawrence Kubie and
the paper in which he discussed creativity and the prison wardens.
It was again one particular paragraph which elicited a response
similar to those I experienced when first encountering the words of
Ronald Fairbairn and Susanne Langer. There was an immediate and

instinctive impression that something of major importance for the understanding of the children's work had just been read, whilst its exact relevance would only become apparent in time. This is what it said:

> The symbolic process is the unique gift and attribute of human mentation, and its most valuable. At the same time that it is essential for all that is creative in human thinking it also is most vulnerable to distortion. (Kubie, 1974, p. 257)

Lawrence Kubie's ideas on how much could go wrong with the symbolisation of experience provide some clarification for the earlier comments on Jung's 'living symbol' and psychoses. His opinion on this issue is one with which I can wholeheartedly concur.

> That from earliest childhood the symbolic process can go off its rails is perhaps the greatest challenge that medicine faces today; because if this did not happen, there could be neither the neurosis nor the psychosis as we know it in the human being. (Kubie, 1959, p. 73)

The importance of Kubie's ideas for the work was that they brought home for the first time the fact that the symbol could function as both a negative and positive factor in the child's growth and development. In so doing he provided the first hint as to where an answer to the children's difficulties might lie. The creative capacity of non-verbal symbolic activity, which had been proclaimed as a major factor in the resolution of these difficulties, was now having to be viewed as a major factor in causing and conserving them.

From there it was only an inch away to deciding that if it was through the symbolisation of experience that things can go so badly wrong, then it would be by activating and utilising that same process that things could be helped to be put right.

And this was thought to have been happening.

Just as the conditions necessary for a safe externalising had evolved, almost inadvertently, as a consequence of a coming together of many different factors, so it seemed that the conditions necessary for some degree of symbolic reconstruction had been arrived at in a similar way.

It was at this point, after what had been a prolonged effort to make some sense of what the children were aspiring to on a symbolic level, that I fell away into writing a rather brief conclusion. Nothing has been added or taken away since I ended the paper thus:

> The final contention is that the environment had become a place where the children were experiencing a peculiarly dynamic and focused opportunity for creative and symbolic expression, which was of benefit to them in several ways.
>
> For many of the children its most immediate value was in its capacity to alleviate the distress associated with their more intolerable concerns whilst offering the prospect of more substantial help to come.
>
> For all of them it assisted in their everyday task of trying to make sense of the world, in their attempt to resolve and reconstruct aspects of it which had been unsatisfactory in the past and, when all was going really well, in constructing something new and better on which to build for the future.

Part III

Companions on the Way

Of the three working relationships to be presented here, two of the children have already been introduced. 'Master Eeps' is the boy who swore a lot. The brevity of the comments on him in no way reflects the value of our time together. David had such a powerful influence on how the room developed that it seems only right to say a lot more about him. I am assisted in this by having kept the notes I wrote during the time we worked together. The boy in 'Two Apples would have been Ideal' is met for the first time. This story goes to the heart of the contentions on feeding and symbolic construction and has been included mainly for that reason. It also shows how a little contact can go a long way.

20

Master Eeps

The boy with the overwhelming need to swear was also fascinated by tiles on ceilings, brackets on pipes and the stitches of sweaters. A possible explanation for these 'interests' was that he had lain for hours unfed and untended to as a baby, with nothing to relate to or to focus on, except the features of the walls and the ceilings. Not every stitch attracted him, but when one did he would approach with enthusiasm and a sort of compulsive delight, take hold of it between his finger and thumb, pull it towards him and exclaim 'eeps', a prolonged sound which seemed to add to the potency of the experience.

It was a sound which many of the other children began to use, mainly as a means of releasing tension, to demonstrate distress, sometimes to express satisfaction with a bobo or with something they had just made, and occasionally to exclaim their delight at an anticipated pleasure. If anything was declared to be 'eepsy' it was in some sense satisfying or satisfactory.

When he left to go to a residential school, the word lingered on for about two years, before becoming a fond memory which was talked about but seldom used. At the height of its popularity I was frequently referred to as Mrs Eeps, a name he had given me, and one which I liked, for obvious reasons. My relationship with this boy was perhaps the most tender of all those I experienced in the room. It was with him that I learned how to hold a child's hand, palm to palm, and suggest, if they were feeling acutely agitated or distressed, they let it 'spill over' to me.

I had taken these words from Frances Tustin's *Autistic States in Children*, which I had read several months before I began setting up the environment. I relocated the book recently and easily found the passage which I must have read so long ago: 'Unbearable bodily tension which is not understood, empathised and relieved by the mother quickly enough is experienced as disturbing "overflow"' (Tustin, 1981, p. 92). And further down the same page:

Work with psychotic children has brought home to me the importance of this 'overflow' – this 'spill-over' of psychological and physiological tension. The child experiences it as tangible body stuff which overflows

83

out of his control. He cannot process it. He recoils from this dangerous stuff in the 'not-me' outside world. Or he may feel possessed by it and be unmanageably hyperactive. In early infancy, the mother's disciplined attitudes and behaviour seem to control, channel and render harmless this overflow which is beyond the child's control. She acts as both analyser and synthesiser, just as the psychoanalyst has to do in a more artificial way later on, if things go wrong. (Ibid.)

On a second reading I also discovered on adjacent pages, and with an acute sense of irony, answers to some of the questions I had been puzzling over since I began the work. I was somewhat consoled by the realisation that even if I had read them years ago, I probably would not have recognised their significance.

Master Eeps was the boy who helped me most to understand the depth of response which would be required if the work with the children was to be at all effective.

This is a picture which he drew of someone reaching up towards the light. It was drawn when he was aged ten years and eight months. He said the figure in it was his father.

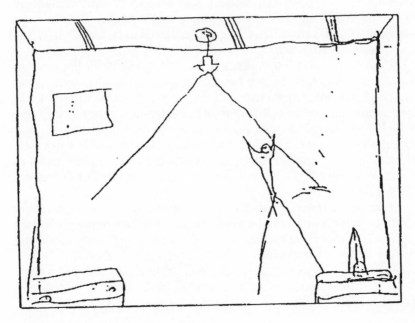

The original drawing was 35 cm x 26 cm

21

THE EARLY DAYS WITH DAVID

If the experience with Master Eeps was the most tender, then the relationship with David was the most prolonged and profound. It was with him that many of the raw practical issues were put through the mangle of experience, in the process of clarifying what were to become the basic procedures in the room. The work took place over the whole period in which the environment was being transformed from a classroom into a therapeutic facility.

The first time I met David was a few days before leaving the unit to go on the course in special educational needs. I can't now recall exactly how much time we initially spent together, but I don't think it was much more than a few hours. I have three early memories of him. One is that he came up to my room and painted a large picture, approximately four feet by three feet, using gloss paint on plywood. It was of two teddy bears, a big one and a smaller one.

Another is of his face, which I think very openly expressed the emotional battering he had experienced. I even have a photograph of him then, which is somewhat perplexing as I can't remember taking it and at that time I only rarely had my camera in the unit. A third, which is more of an image than a memory, is of the very marked discrepancy between the expression in each of his eyes. This began to fade away gradually until, several months after we started working together, both eyes looked very similar. David's liking for having his photograph taken gave me a relatively unintrusive way of noting such changes.

The next time we met was a year later, when I returned from the course. I was overflowing with enthusiasm about the potential benefits of using sand trays and convinced that, given the opportunity, a new and more effective way of working should be possible. That opportunity came with David.

As the context in which we began to work had a substantial effect on our progress, something of its character needs to be explained. In the months before my return, David had succeeded in antagonising almost all the staff in the unit and, during discussions about his future, their declared preference was for his complete removal from it as soon as possible. An administrator in the child guidance

service in overall charge of the unit, and the educational psychologist responsible for the case were less certain about what to do with
him next. They felt inclined, if at all possible, to persevere and keep
him there. This predicament for them coincided with my readiness
for a challenge and I was promised their full support if I attempted
to work with David.

It was not long after this that I began to experience the cold under-
currents of having gone against the group's wishes, an act which,
at a later stage of the work, probably contributed to its demise.

The severity of David's difficulties, and the fact that there were
four other children in the room, resulted in this being one of the
most unsatisfactory times for the children. No one got the attention
they needed and deserved. It was also one of the hardest times for
me, as I was attempting to fulfil two basically incompatible roles in
which the children were getting neither a teacher nor a therapist.
To varying degrees this situation was a detrimental factor in my
capacity to function effectively throughout the duration of the work.

What follows are most of the notes which were kept during those
early days with David. They were written down at the end of each
day, usually while travelling on a bus or an underground train across
the city. They were used mainly as a means of trying to make sense
of what had been happening during the day and of offloading some
of the torments.

They are intended to give a sense of the delights and dilemmas
experienced at that time. To make them easier to read a few of the
words have been changed but the facts are unaltered. Some details
of David's life and of the murder have been omitted. They were felt
to be too personal and would not have contributed in any way to
the purpose of this account.

David was on a temporary suspension from the unit when I
returned from the course and, as the dates will suggest, he was rein-
troduced to it on a part-time basis.

The following series of six small undated pictures were found in
a book after David had moved on to another school. They were
drawn while I was away on the course and he was with another
teacher. He must have been eight years old at the time. They are
used here to introduce the various members of his family. The
original drawings were 16.5 cm x 10 cm.

David

David and his father

Brother Peter

Sister T.

The older sister

The sister who was rarely mentioned

April 25th

David tells me of a boy who threw a baby from a high-rise flat. The boy had also thrown bottles from it. A woman from the children's home, where he used to live, had told him the story. He said that everyone in his house that morning had heard a voice saying 'come on get up', but that no one was there. And there was no one living near who could have said it. He showed me a scab on his leg and said his Dad had got cream for it. He drew a picture of a storm, with lightning cracking a house, leaves coming off a tree, and a woman with an umbrella.[8]

this walking by and shes putting up her umbrella

the lightnings going on to the tree and the leaves are dropping and then its struck the house and it cracked all the house and smashed all the windows

The original drawing was 20 cm x 16 cm   11 years 9 months

April 26th

David threw marbles into some water. I asked him to stop. He wasn't pleased and got so angry he looked as if he might throw me in next.

May 1st

David drew three pictures and asked to play in the sand. He left what he was doing and went to have a game of snooker with his father

---

[8] This was one of over 250 drawings which he produced throughout the whole time he used the room. It is being included because it probably epitomised David's state of mind at the beginning of our work together. It was probably more representative of mine by the end of it.

who was visiting the unit. As I was dismantling the tray I saw that he had made a wall in one of the corners, using sand and blocks. Water has been poured in behind it. He knows that these particular blocks should not be used in wet sand. He returns and decides to make another tray. He begins to put the blocks back in and I remind him that they are not to be put in with water. He becomes angry and throws one onto the floor. He swears at me but recovers quickly; I take longer.[9]

May 8th

David makes another tray. He places two gorillas in a cage and puts a fence on top. He tells me he is bored.[10] He is very tense. I say I think he has a lot of things worrying him and he is keeping them packed inside. He seems to accept this and is quite calm. There have been several brief but very intense incidents today. David mocked my voice and flicked milk at me. He threw a protractor on the floor and refused, for a moment only, to go to the playroom. He was very disappointed not to be allowed out to play football in the playground at lunchtime. This decision was not mine so I was not seen as the great depriver.

David was very cruel to another boy who was upset. He grabbed his foot with great strength and relish and squeezed and twisted it with both hands. He then flexed his arm to demonstrate the size of his muscles and said 'strength'.

May 9th

David says he is bored. When he didn't get a game of snooker on the 'big' table he came back to the room and threw a box of crayons across it. He then pushed over a large box of blocks and threw a box of dominoes.

---

[9] There were not enough materials in the room at this time to leave a tray construction in place for an indeterminate period. This was later remedied. It was an accepted limit not to put these particular blocks into the sand trays. As with all other limits, having to establish it with David was very difficult. He viewed any withholding of any kind as a lack of caring on my part. I did not realise this fully at the time.

[10] This becomes a statement of some significance, and not only with him. It is a phrase which is used often by the children and usually precedes a mood of extreme unrest.

Later, when I went out of the room to fill the kettle with water, David twisted another boy's arm and kicked him. He also took a gun from the same boy and when I asked him to give it back he threw it in his face. David then left the room saying he was not coming back in and that he would run away.

May 10th

David was looking absolutely miserable. He said his sister T. had been chased home by a drunk man. His father had been angry because she was late and he had been shouting at her. David was worried about what information the school would be passing on to his father when he visited this week. Although I will not be seeing his father I assure David that my 'official' comment, which will be passed on, is that we have had quite a difficult week but are now beginning to get down to work on some of the things that have been troubling him.[11]

I asked if he had anything else worrying him. He said that his previous teacher in the unit knew about it. I assumed he was referring to the murder and we just left it there. As I had been on playground duty I was able to take him out with me. There had been no problems and he was pleased to have been out.

May 14th

David picked up a screwdriver and poked it at another boy. I asked him to put it down. He said no and danced around the table brandishing it. I asked him again to give it to me and he did. Later he decided not to have a swim with the others because the water was too cold. Then he got in and enjoyed it thoroughly. His whole body is remarkably tense.

At the morning break he sat comfortably alongside me on one of the big chairs until he'd finished drinking his milk. He moved away easily. He went to the playroom at the end of the morning and

---

[11] Contact with David's father and work with the family was the joint responsibility of the head teacher, the educational psychologist and the social worker. I reported to them on our progress and on any concerns I might have about his general welfare. The only time I ever recall talking to David's father was during a trip by car to look over the residential school which David moved to, after his time in the unit.

returned to the room very overheated, emotionally and physically.[12]
I suggested that he might like to cool down in the room adjacent to
mine which is not being used at present. He was able to do this and
came back in looking pink and quiet. He told me, while drawing on
the cover of his English book, that he had nearly got kept in for a
month by his father. As he was talking I placed a clean piece of paper
under his pen. He said that he and his big brother Peter had gone
back to their old children's home the night before last. They had
smashed things up and wouldn't do as they were asked by the staff
there. The home had phoned his father the next morning. David
offered this as the reason he had been upset yesterday. He had been
frightened his Dad would beat him up.

The 'upset' he was referring to concerned an incident in which he
had thrown a carton of milk across the staffroom.

He had been told by his father never to go to the home again.
David made two trays. This is the story for the first one.

'The wee woman's got all the medicine with her. The men are going to
be working. It's dead sunny and all the beach has dried up. The horses are
trying to get a shade underneath the trees. Granny's took an electric shock
and the doctor came and had to put her in bed.'
Look I put in the wee streetlights.

The second tray consisted mainly of domestic animals fenced off
and penned in. It looked as if several horses were drinking water
from a pool.[13]

May 16th

Last night David's father had given Peter £2 to go to the shows (the
fairground). Later, when David found out about this he asked if he
could also have some money. His father gave him 10p and sent him
to the shops for a 'message'. He was told he could keep the change.
There was only 2p left so David threw away the 10p and the 2p.

He said his Dad was always telling him to get out of the living-
room and to get his hands off the video. He is convinced his father

---

[12] The playroom was usually supervised by two auxiliary workers. The equipment
available for use included mats, a few benches, a large plastic barrel, a tyre on wheels
and various pieces of smaller apparatus.
[13] These are the only trays which were mentioned in the notes.

likes Peter much better than he likes him. He hadn't slept well and seemed very fed up.

There was trouble in the 'quiet room' at lunchtime.[14] David had thrown a marble and kicked a bucket. Later in the day he accused me of allowing another boy in the group to do things I wouldn't let him do. (This boy is also called Peter.) I suggested to David that this situation reminded him of his Dad and his brother and that he was implying that I liked 'our' Peter better than I liked him. This amused him.

May 20th

It is brother Peter's birthday this week. David says he will get him a bundle of crap because his brother is crap. Peter had already received a present of a skateboard and had kept it to himself. David was hiding in the 'cabin' this morning. He said while he had been in there he had been listening to 'our' Peter talking to himself. When he came out of the cabin he began cutting a large leaf and the stalk of a plant. I gently asked him not to. He gently continued. I suggested that something was troubling him and maybe we could talk about it. He stopped cutting the plant but didn't talk.

Our Peter has now become a focus for David's negative feelings about his brother. They have had several arguments today and have been spitting and calling each other names. David threw a pair of scissors at him with little attempt to safely direct their flight. He watched Peter draw a cross with a snake wrapped around it. He then made nine unsuccessful attempts to copy it before giving up and scrawling all over the page.

May 21st

David was very 'edgy' again today and got angry when I said he couldn't use the saw.[15] When I was out for my break he went down to the secretary's room. When I was called to attend to him he was

---

[14] The quiet room was a place in which children who were not going out to play at intervals and lunchtime could go for activities such as playing board games and reading stories.

[15] Woodwork was one of the activities we did as a class and there was a workbench available for this in one of the other rooms. The saw was used occasionally in our room for such tasks as adjusting the height of a table, and later on for making trays.

under a chair. I discovered he had been sliding around the floor under the chairs. He was curled up and was murmuring 'fucking, fucking, fucking'. He would have come out gradually but I chose to haul him rather than talk him out as his behaviour was producing such an extreme response in two of the surrounding adults. I wanted him out of there and back upstairs as quickly as possible. While I was on the course there had apparently been several incidents in the school office. During one of these he had entered it carrying a burning comic. I never asked for any other details.

Although he knew he wasn't allowed to go out to the playground on that particular day, it seems that soon after I had left the room he had asked the worker who was temporarily in charge of the group for permission to do so. When she refused he left anyway. He'd also left other things. Later I noticed there was paint high up on the walls and on the ceiling and I discovered that he had thrown numerous objects on the floor, even Teddy.[16]

May 22nd

Today David brought in a photograph of brother Peter. He tore it up and stuck it together again; then he painted the back of it yellow, muttering several times as he did so in the kind of strange high voice he had used under the office chairs yesterday. The words on this occasion were 'I've fixed my brother.' I had never met his brother and this was the first time I had seen a picture of him. Peter was a year older but he looked much, much bigger and not at all like David.

David seemed to be extremely concerned about the possibility of his father finding out that he had been climbing on a wall. [I have not recorded which wall or when.] He said that once before when he had climbed a wall his father had hit him in the face. He was very upset and later lay against Teddy crying quietly. He spent almost thirty minutes lying there, then did some woodwork very happily. We talked again about how important it was that we worked things out between us.

---

[16] This was a large brown teddy bear, about three feet six inches high, which had been given to the class group while we were on a visit to a Charity Film Performance. It was very popular with the children and got 'fed' and cuddled often. There were a few other small soft toys and dolls in the room but these were rarely used.

May 25th

Today David played with our Peter. They were both delighted, laughing a lot and making houses with clay by rolling it into logs. 'See my cracking ideas', he said to Peter, as he cut a door in the clay. He added, 'Miss, I used to do that with plasticine.' I asked when that was. He replied, 'Ages ago when I was in the other school.'

At the lunch table he was very agitated and touched his throat several times with his knife. On one occasion, still with the knife, he moved away from the table. After lunch I was not on duty so I went up to the room with him and stayed there. He continued working with the clay. He said he would be alone in the house with his father that night. His sister T. was going to stay with her pal and Peter would be staying with his.

He is obviously very frightened at the thought of being alone with his father. Much of his recent unsettled behaviour stems from this fear. He resists all encouragement to talk more about what else is troubling him.

In the morning, after the pleasant early start with Peter, they began to over-excite each other. While I was washing a brush David had poured dirty water over another boy's painting. When I returned he had hidden under the chair. I said that making a mess of someone's work wasn't acceptable. I cleaned up a bit and while I was doing this David got out from under the chair and challenged me about something else. He was angry and although not in full flight, he broke the large wooden sculpture of a man which he and I had been working on by jumping at it with both feet.

Before it was broken he threw a block at it and then left the room to suck at the tube on the fire extinguisher. These acts were delighting Peter. I was less enamoured with them. I now realise that David is nowhere near being ready to work co-operatively with another child. Peter was trying all the time to draw him into unacceptable activities. Until he gets stronger I will need to be firmer about keeping him out of situations which put him under too much stress.

David's finale was to push over a large tub of black water again, in the direction of a painting belonging to another child. This made an awful mess. The days of the messes are gathering pace. I found one yesterday as I was going downstairs. He had made it with a large pile of dirty paper towels as he was leaving the building to go home. This seemed to be a favourite time for him. I assumed when he got home he would have no choice but to be a good clean boy. On leaving the unit today he jumped onto a fence in mock chase of another boy, then, as I was about to reprimand him, he quietly got into his taxi.

Today I told David that there was no need for his father to keep coming into the unit. We were now getting on well with the work and in future the educational psychologist would arrange to meet his father in the local clinic. After several attempts the educational psychologist has decided that work with the father, with or without David or other members of the family present, offers little hope of success.

As the day has shown, the lid on what needs to come out is gradually coming off with more abandon. I anticipate that the new arrangements about his father will precipitate the release.

May 28th

A fight began when David threw biscuits into another boy's face and shouted 'black bastard' over and over again. He ran out of the room and then returned to adopt a crouching position at the door. I feebly suggested that he must be feeling angry or unhappy about something. He came in a few minutes later and began talking through what was troubling him.

His grandfather had died. His sister had found out. He was uncertain whose father it was. He was reluctant to work. Sitting together at the big desk I said there was something we could do instead. This was my first ever attempt at a version of the Squiggle Game. I drew a line and then he drew one. After taking turns we finished a drawing. I put in an eye and he smiled. We did another. I drew what looked like the top of a head and the top line of a beak. After a few more lines it became a bird. When we had finished this one he turned and said, 'I'll do my work now.'

Later in the morning there was another unhappy incident. This one was precipitated by me. Peter and David were using the clay again. Without me noticing they had begun to paint the wet clay with black paint. This was not allowed, mostly because the clay couldn't be used again if it was decided not to let it dry out. It wasn't what I said, it was that I spoke with a harsh voice. David responded with alarm as though I had wounded him and he very quickly attempted to defend himself by retaliating with abusive comments.

He threw one of the clay objects on to the ceiling and splattered another onto the floor.

I was irritated by the clay on the ceiling. He sensed this and it soon became apparent that the mess-making was about to be substantially escalated. I had to hold his hands and insist that I was going to stop him making things any worse, for him and for me! What began as a serious tussle became slightly good-humoured. We were able to settle down and talk about his grandfather dying. I asked if there were other people who had died or gone away. 'Aye', he said, 'the woman my Dad killed. My grandmother. My Mum left us.'

We talked about how all these things happening must have made him feel very sad. The rest of the day was good.

May 29th

David said the sunshine came into his bedroom in the mornings. I had to physically restrain him from breaking up the wooden sculpture again. This time he attempted it with a long stick. As I did so he told me how he hated his Dad, because it was his Dad's fault that they had been put in a home. It again became a very good-natured sort of holding and he would probably have talked a lot more but Peter and another boy in the group began arguing. They were getting close to hitting each other so I had to leave David to intervene with them.

As I was preventing Peter from assaulting the other boy, I got dragged under a desk. At this point David began jumping around the room and throwing things. He threw a pen which bounced off one of the lights and broke the light shade. This precipitated a further loss of control. He grabbed my camera and began dancing around with it. I heard myself yelling at him to put it down before I was able to take a deep breath and firmly ask him to do so. He quietened down. I don't think it was anything I said. When I asked him to clear up he did.

I returned to talk with Peter and we were getting on fine until I looked up and saw David climbing out of the window. Suddenly only his head and the top part of his body were in view. He was actually dangling there approximately 100 feet above the ground. Fortunately he had extremely strong arms!

When I reached him I said that this was exactly the kind of behaviour which would lead me to contact his father and that if he

didn't get back into the room immediately I would do just that.[17]
He climbed back in very quickly indeed and was relaxed and quiet
for the rest of the morning. He did some class work at the interval
and then played with the clay.

David is obviously beginning to contrive situations in which I
have to hold him. I will need to find a way to pre-empt this otherwise
there will be some unproductive and strenuous days ahead.

May 31st

The educational psychologist had apparently phoned David's home
yesterday to speak to his Dad but he had been out. David suggested
he had phoned because I had told him about the broken light. This
was a test I easily passed as I hadn't told anyone. He was just as easily
convinced. He admitted to being troubled about something but he
said his big sister had told him not to tell anyone. His father had
been drinking at the pub last night. He and Peter had gone to bed
but had been frightened he would come home drunk and hit them.
We talked once more about how important it was that he learned
to trust me with his concerns. He said he could.

June 3rd

When David came in he said he had had a good weekend and he
seemed to be at ease. He did his work reluctantly. He had a good
playtime although he played with his hands in his pockets. He had
something in them but I didn't ask what it was. He also seemed to
be rather tired. After his return to the classroom he went downstairs
to play snooker with another boy from the class. After about twenty
minutes I heard him on the stairs swearing and shouting names. I
asked him to come inside the room to sort things out and he came.
He said the other boy had been losing and had thrown the snooker

---

[17] This may not have been the correct thing to do therapeutically in these circumstances but I had great difficulty in not fainting on the floor, and it did work. I should
confess to having a profound fear of heights. This incident was one of the most
memorable occasions on which I resorted to using David's fear of his father to control
him. There was another when he climbed onto the roof of a shed in the playground
and began to throw slates down at the other children. In those situations children
are usually careful to aim for the spaces. It had not been so on this occasion.

balls and told him to fuck off, so he had taken the balls back downstairs to be put away and said he wasn't going to play.

He wasn't settled and began making a mess of another boy's sand tray. He then attempted to squeeze blue paint from one tube into another of green paint. Keeping his hands under the table he also surreptitiously cut up a clay medallion he had been making. In this messy mood he had gone into one of the unused rooms and had begun to damage a polystyrene ball by tearing at it. I followed him in there. I said I would stop him breaking anything else.

He took me over to where a clay plate had been smashed on the floor. It had probably been broken the previous Friday. It was a present he had received from a girl during his recent visit to his old children's home. I suggested that perhaps he had broken it and wanted me to know. He said this was so. I also suggested that he may have done it on Friday before he went home because he knew he would have to be 'good' all weekend. I added that I thought he often made messes before leaving the unit. This was also accepted.

On the way back to the room he grabbed a piece of wood and threatened to throw it. He was just teasing me!

There was obviously something else troubling him. I firmly asserted this and said we would spend some time together later. I would have talked with him then but two of the other children began arguing and I had to move quickly to attend to them.

When he came down to lunch he informed me he had made another mess but had then cleared it up. When I checked out what had happened I discovered paint had been splashed around. The photograph of brother Peter was ruined and he had scratched across the eyes and the mouth of a photograph of one of the other children.

We all went outside later for some fresh air and he threatened to run away with the others – but didn't.

When all this messing around had quietened down I sat down feeling tired and complained that I had had an awful day and that there was a limit to what I could do to help them when they were all jumping about so much. David seemed to be genuinely sorry and said he was.

Before going home he got under a chair and it was again apparent that he wanted to tell me something but was unable to do so. I gave him as much encouragement as I could but he said he would keep it to himself for another day.

We talked again about him feeling that his life was in a mess and that the messes he made were a way of letting that be known. I again stressed that we needed to find a way of talking about what was troubling him before he began acting it out. He then said he had been upset about scratching the photograph and breaking the plate. He took my hand like a little boy as we went downstairs and was at ease as he left for home.

June 4th

Yesterday David told me that his father had stayed out the previous night and that he and Peter were worried again but their big sister had been there to look after them. Last night his father had been five hours late for tea and suggested that David and his brother should get out of bed and scramble for some money. They didn't want to get up so he gave the money to his sister instead. David said, 'See that boy that followed my sister up to the door, my Dad was going to fight him.'

His father had told him about two men who had committed suicide. One strangled himself out of a window and another put his head down the toilet. He told me about all the women who were being raped up his bit and about a wee girl enticed by a flasher who then hit her on the back of the neck. As he was telling me all this David was sorting out the paper money into bundles and was thoroughly enjoying doing it. He finished sorting it out and then did his work.

By lunchtime he was agitated again and on the way down to the dining-room asked if he could invite someone to the table. I said I would prefer him not to and explained why. He was angry and after climbing up a water pipe and hanging from a ledge he ran shouting out of a side door. I went to talk to him and explained again that I didn't want anyone from another class to visit our table when several of the children in the group, including himself, were so unsettled.

He came back in, sat down at the table and settled for for a while. He was still very agitated and soon began whistling. He then poured a lot of salt on his dinner. I asked if he'd let me help sort out what was troubling him. I said I needed his help to do this. He looked sad and I tapped his foot several times with mine underneath the table. He relaxed a little.

I had to leave him to begin my playground duty and he was told to join me when he had finished his lunch. When I left he had become very cheeky to the dinner lady and to one of the staff. He came out to the playground shouting. He then went off somewhere, found a broken bottle and came back with it. He threw a few pieces of stone around but then came over and sat on the bench beside me.

He said he wanted to climb onto a roof to find a nest and kill the wee birds. He said he had set fire to a paper in the classroom. Then he said he hadn't. He had handed me two matches and a bashed cigarette in the morning. He threatened to run away several times but stayed. Going back up to the classroom he took hold of my hand.

Peter was goading him when we were back in class but David remained calm and was settled enough to take his turn for baking. This pleased him very much.

June 6th

David came in looking tired and it was soon very clear how troubled he was. His father had been drinking and dancing and falling around. David had wanted to go to bed but wasn't allowed to. Then and later he said he hated his father and wished he was back in prison. His said his sisters would like that too. He had several angry outbursts cursing his father and wishing he would go away.

There were a series of incidents throughout the day but they were a bit more controlled than most of those he had had before. A large pack of paper towels were thrown, a stick was brandished and cracked against a chair, he sucked water out of the fire extinguisher and went into another room and sucked one there.

I made the mistake early this morning of letting him go for a walk in the playground. It was another calculated risk. He went to the office and was removed physically by the woman who can't like him. He may well have gone there to talk to her. She was often there at that time of the day. Whatever happened it may well have provoked the day's events.

David sat in one of the sand trays and poured sand over his legs and lower body. At playtime in the quiet room he had a fight and came into the playground with his fist raised above his head behaving as if he had just triumphed at something. Throughout the day I had to hold him several times to prevent him from messing up too many things. Approaching lunchtime he began kicking at the kettle. He lay over the big table and kicked and when I was restraining him I thought I'd hurt his arm. He began to cry. I am not sure if it was from that hurt or from hurt inside. He cried quietly. Later when I asked if I had hurt him he said no.

He continued to cry quietly and I got him a hanky and offered him an apple. I put it beside him. He refused the apple but took it home later with a carton of milk. Several times during the day he said he wished he was in a residential school. He said if his Dad went back to prison they could all live with his oldest sister who had her own house. He also said he was going to do things at school which would require him to be put in a residential school.

Several times yesterday and today he said he was going to run away. I assumed that someone at home was threatening to plan his future for him.

In the group discussion which is becoming a regular feature of the morning routine everyone said that David probably feels I don't love him if I raise my voice or get angry. They all say that they feel exactly the same with their mothers at home. I say I'll try to stop it immediately.

It was our day for visiting the adventure playground. On the bus going there David began to say 'shite, shite, shite' because I wouldn't let him sit in the front seat. He quietened down and then got very excited talking with two of the girls who help out there. Then he had an excellent time. He told me he had a cigarette and a match. Then he said he hadn't. He said he had stolen 5p from his father's pocket while he was in the bathroom. Then he said he hadn't. He made a clay dish. Then he broke it. Then he wanted to make another but there wasn't enough time.

June 7th

David was fine when he came in. He said he'd been at a disco. He told a story of a slate falling onto his sister's nose and face. This had happened before he was put away into the children's home. David had scratched his finger with a knife in the dining-room yesterday. He told his father he had got it playing football. His Dad was coming to collect him from school at the end of the day and take him to a meeting with the educational psychologist at the local clinic.

He was trying very hard to be 'good', but keeping things under control, even for his father, is becoming increasingly difficult. In the course of the day he knocked things over in another child's tray, cut up a pad of paper into small pieces and threw cartons on the floor.

He had a very rejecting experience with a member of staff outside the room during the morning, and he felt hurt and angry for the remainder of the day. He very quietly spoke her name and made faces as he did so. His expressions were odd and rather clown-like. During lunch he picked up a knife and threatened another child.

I was in a very impatient and troubled mood myself and failed to help him. He was pushing in every direction and I felt irritated and rejecting. I said I was fed up. I was glad when his father arrived. I'd had enough for the week.

June 10th

We talked about the visit to the psychologist the previous Friday. He said it had been OK. He had matches. They were troubling him. He wanted me to know about them. He commented that I was looking tired. He told the boy he likes best that his Dad had been in jail for killing someone and that he wished he was back in there because he was always battering him around.

We had several confrontations about his behaviour but we got back together after only brief episodes at sea. He is beginning to tolerate a lot more ordinary discipline.

June 11th

David had told the head of the unit that his Dad was going away for two days and that he wasn't supposed to tell anyone. This has been a really good day for him.

June 12th

The notes from today are lying in the street somewhere. I must have dropped them! I was very clumsy and impatient again today and caused David some unnecessary upset. This is probably the first time he tried to deal with my mess.

Another child related a dream and David told one of his. A tarantula and all its wee babies were attacking him in bed. When he woke up in the morning his arms were all cut. He called his Dad who came and said it wouldn't happen again.

June 13th

On another visit to the adventure playground David got excited and delighted when he was being chased by one of the workers there. He made an excellent clay pot. He needed some help to quieten down but it was a pleasant interaction.

David's Dad had been drunk again last night. He had insisted that he and Peter should get out of bed to listen to the sound of footsteps. He said he had heard the door creaking and rattling.

After being told by me that he could not dismantle a toy I had brought in, he threw marbles and an Action Man across the room. He then messed up the paints and began throwing cardboard shapes around. This was certainly another difficult day. There was a further episode of messing and throwing things around. He then began to clear up spontaneously.

June 14th

David had a very controlled day. He told me his Dad had come in drunk again and said he would give David and Peter £1 each if they would go into the room where the noises were for five minutes. Later I spent time with him in the staffroom during my break. It was empty, warm and quiet there. I asked if he would like to talk about the things that had happened a long time ago. He said he didn't want to. I asked why he thought his Dad kept talking about the noises. He said he didn't know but that he was really scared and his sister's legs were bruised where he had been hanging on to her. She had kept hitting him to try to get him off.

David 'dismantled' the room at lunchtime in a magnificent effort to clean it all. He even swept the carpets. When I entered I got a shock and my initial response upset him. It took me a long time to satisfactorily explain my preliminary alarm. As we were sitting talking at either side of a table David began scraping at a join in the wood. Before I said anything he suggested he was being destructive. We didn't take that any further. With no apparent lead up to it he said his mother used to hit him every morning because he wet the bed. We spoke about children wetting the bed. He said they did that when they had troubles. He also said that when his mother battered him, his Dad would batter her.[18]

---

[18] This may well have been his father's version of what had happened and not David's memory of it.

At home-time David climbed a fence looking for a bird's nest. When he got down he ran off. The woman taxi-driver who usually takes him home, and with whom he has an excellent relationship, told him to get into the cab and settled him down. She had told me to leave it to her and I did.

June 17th

David tells me about a friend who runs away, steals money, is battered, put in pyjamas, and then runs away again. He was upset about it and seems to have been involved in some way. There are more stories about drinking in the house. There is a woman in the house now. He doesn't say if she is living there or just visiting.

June 18th

Throughout the day David found it hard to hold on. I had to spend a lot of time with him and this was unfair to the others. They were often very understanding and patient with me. Circumstances at home are extremely difficult for him. He again expressed his feelings about his Dad and how much he hates him. He said he had taken money from his Dad's pocket when he was drunk and that he would run away with his wee pal.

There seems to be little hope of my being able to work with him while conditions in the house are so unsettled. His fears about what his father might do are pervading his whole life. I assume the presence of the woman is a significant factor in this.

Today he mentioned the sister he'd drawn as a fish. He has never mentioned her before. She is sixteen. She leaves the house in the morning and comes back at 10.30 p.m. She seems to do nothing around the house.

David was hitting the light switches with a piece of wood and succeeded in breaking one. If I hadn't got hold of him and the piece of wood he would have broken more. I found it difficult today not to react to his provocation. On one occasion when I held him he spat and spat and spat and then tried to rub his head in it.

There has been more drinking in the house. His father had 'jokingly' said he was going to hit one of David's sisters over the head with a bottle. He said his father had hit him and then given him some money. He had been late to bed again and had been scared.

June 19th

Today I was on the verge of calling a taxi and sending David home as I was unable to make any contact with him. He had broken part of a window yesterday but was unable to tell me about it. The drinking continues. Something had happened at the pub which had made his father very angry. David didn't know what it was.

Everyone in the group had a major upset today. After the storm had passed David began to describe something which he said had happened a long time ago. He said they had all been covered in blood and had gone to the hospital. His father had been pushing him and his brother off the mantel shelf and had put Peter's foot in the fire.

He then spoke in some detail about the night the woman had been murdered. This was the first time he had spoken about it and he did so in a very quiet and easy way. It was a half day and he had begun talking just a few minutes before it was time to go downstairs. He remained calm in spite of several other disruptions in the group and was one of the few that day who was able to settle for lunch and leave calmly in the taxi.

June 20th

It is obvious from David's behaviour that the broken window is troubling him greatly. He has tried without much conviction to blame another boy. Frieze paper on the wall has been messed up and a jar of water poured over a table. David stayed out on the stairs and was hitting the light switches with a piece of slate. I encouraged him to come into the room.

Eventually I laid it on the line that I could be absolutely no help to him if he wouldn't tell me what was troubling him. He came in and sat at his desk. He had smeared the inside with red paint. His Dad was working again today. He said he had done something. Then he added that he knew he hadn't broken the glass.

He kept his jacket on. He made a mosaic with white plastic squares. He squeezed milk all over the puppet theatre. When we were able to talk again he said that his Dad had kicked him and that he was always getting the blame. He began thumping his head into an adjacent sand tray. He threw some sand around and kept insisting that he had not broken the window.

A little later he told me he had broken the window.

He had got kicked by his father last night because he'd been playing dummy fighting. He had told his Dad we were all mean to him at school and his Dad had said he knew we were mean.

David left the room again. This time he went out with another boy who was glad to be distracted from his class work. When he did return he came to sit near me but was still upset and began tearing paper into small pieces and throwing it on the floor and at other people. Later in the playground he tore his T-shirt into pieces and then wiped up some of the dirt. He said he was cleaning the playground. Gradually he began to calm down and by the afternoon he was playing a very amicable game of cops and robbers with a small boy who was visiting from another group.

June 21st

David said his father had been chasing his sister around the house with his teeth out.

June 24th

I have decided I want to stop writing these notes. I am tired of it all. It has really worn me down. To do this kind of work with a child like David needs a lot more support and a lot more understanding from the people around. I am really fed up and of course I am showing it and that is making him worse.

And so it was, in this disheartened mood, just a few days before the beginning of the summer holidays, I gave up writing anything about the day's events. This was undoubtedly a crisis time for me and I doubt if I would have been able to continue containing David's distress for much longer. But, with an ease which can only be achieved with the passage of time, it is now possible to put what happened then into a more positive context.

As declared at the beginning of this account, one of the main purposes of the notes was to attempt to cast off some of the problems of the day. Consequently there is an unadulterated emphasis on all the things that went wrong and this needs to be fully appreciated.

But, in the midst of all the testing and acting-out, David was spending increasing amounts of time each day drawing, talking, making trays and working creatively with almost every other material available to him in the room. Much time and energy was also being devoted to assisting him in the task of finding the words to describe what was troubling him. He was another of the many children whose difficulty with this was only belatedly grasped.

After the holidays there was a further deluge of difficulties but these were faced with an increased energy and resolve. The moves towards making the environment available for the use of all the children in the unit were slow in coming but were sufficient to keep alive the hope for a better way of working.

Looking back, the biggest regret I have is that the materials and procedures which David did so much to pioneer, and which were subsequently found to be so crucial in helping to keep both the child and the worker afloat during some of their more difficult times, could not have been in place when he needed them.

If this work ever gets off the ground it will be important to let him know of his contribution to it.

22

Two Apples would have been Ideal

There was a tray in the room in which I kept apples, oranges and crisps. This was placed on top of a cupboard and was above eye-level for most of the children. They knew what was usually in it but would have needed to climb onto a low table to make certain. Each morning in the unit a child, chosen from one of the class groups, brought fruit and crisps around to each of the rooms. This was my main supply of solid food. There were many interesting interactions associated with the giving out of food. The one I have chosen to write about relates to an apple.

A boy who had been adopted, and who in his drawings often depicted himself as a robot, made use of the room in phases. On his first visit he made a tray in which wild animals and dinosaurs were biting into each other's mouths and bodies. He often kept his own mouth tightly closed, with his bottom lip tucked tight under the top one, so that his teeth were kept firmly out of sight. When he moved around the room objects seemed to fall off surfaces as he approached and he had great difficulty keeping his elbows and knees away from making quite sharp contact with people and the furniture.

The length of his visits varied but they were similar in tone to those made by the other children. Sometimes I would see him several times a week and then hardly at all for a month. Apart from the more typical visits, there were others which were peculiar to him.

He certainly held the record for the shortest ones ever made. Some of these lasted for about ten seconds. They consisted of his coming to the door of the room and standing there until I was looking directly at him. Once we had silently acknowledged each other's existence, he would say, 'I think I'll just go back down to class and do my work.' I think that on most of these occasions he just needed to check that I was there and available for use, if and when required. Similar kinds of visits were those in which he would come to the door, ask for a bobo, drink the milk while leaning on a low cupboard just inside the room, again look at me very firmly, and then go back to his class without saying anything.

He also loved long, dark, indulgent stays, when he could take his favourite object, an ewok, into the small den which had been set up

109

for him. This had been made by placing a thick cover over a small table and putting a piece of deep foam-rubber on the floor. And there were occasions when he had duped his teacher into thinking he had something to sort out, or that he had an important idea for a tray. His real interest at these times was to check if Ann, a girl he liked very much, was in the room. She had been in his class group before, sadly for him, being moved on to another. There was a further series of such visits when his best friend John was also moved on to a different class.

As he well knew, however, using the room as a general meeting place for friends was not one of its accepted purposes and each time his intentions became clear he was very easily persuaded that there were other ways and means of arranging to be with them. He would return to his class, usually with good humour.

As our relationship was quite trusting but rather distant I was surprised one day when he quite formally told me he had decided I would be the best person to talk to about some old memories which had been coming back to him. He sat beside me at the big desk and I wrote them down, alongside one of the robots which featured so prominently in his drawings.

This is the picture he produced. He was aged nine years and six months at the time. The words he spoke have been printed below for easier reading.

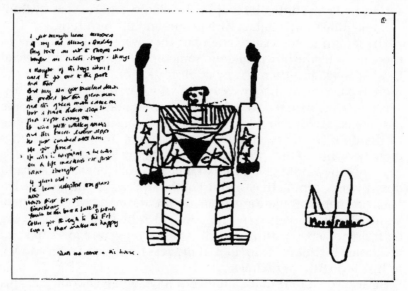

The original drawing was 16.5 cm x 10 cm   9 years 6 months

I just brought back memories of my old Mummy and Daddy. They took me out to shops and bought me sweets and toys and things. I thought of the toys when I used to go out to the park and that.

And my Da got knocked down. He pressed for the green man and the green man came on but a truck didn't stop it just kept coming on. He was just walking across and the truck didn't stop – he just crashed into him.

He got fined.

He was in hospital and he was on a life machine and it just went straight.

[I was] four years old. I've been adopted six years now.

How's that for you?

Excellent.

You'll be the best to talk to.

Celtic got through to the Scottish FA Cup and that makes me happy.

That's my robot in the hoose.

Of all the very strong feelings he experienced, some of the most painful were those associated with having been, in his opinion, the victim of an intolerable injustice. These injustices had usually occurred in relation to one of the other children in his class group, and from the moment he came into the room it was obvious that he was coming right for me, with the purpose of letting me know all about it.

Even during the short journey from the door across the room to where I was positioned, I could sense the build-up of anger. I assumed it had been gaining in intensity from the moment the door of his classroom had closed behind him and he had begun making his way up the two flights of stairs which led to the room.

It was on just such a day that the incident with the apple took place. In my opinion it was a follow-on from something which had happened outside the unit and this will be described first. I will refer to him as 'Paul'.

A group of the children from the unit had been invited, along with hundreds of others from various schools throughout the city, to attend a party given by a local charitable organisation. The food was anticipated with relish but the most exciting prospect was undoubtedly the disco dancing.

Paul and his best friends, John and Ann, were among those chosen to go to the ball. There was some friendly rivalry between the boys as to which of them would get the most dances with Ann. The general consensus was that Paul was her official partner.

In between the food being eaten and the ice cream being dished out the boys took turns dancing with her, but, as the afternoon proceeded and she began to show a marked preference for being with John, the rivalry became more pronounced and much less friendly. At one point, her refusal to dance with Paul ended up with his retreating in a deep mood into the boy's toilet, and refusing to come out. I saw what had happened from a distance and, aware of his distress, I loitered around the entrance, trying to lure him out each time the door swung open.

When he finally emerged after about ten minutes, he was bereft. As I sat down beside him to try to help, he was unable to stop himself from weeping in an overwhelmingly inconsolable way. It was obvious that the experience had opened up a well of distress which was far deeper than anything he might have felt from the loss of the girl. It just poured out of him. The pain was tangible. It was received with words of benign comfort but not spoken about in any specific way. It produced an immediate change in how we both viewed and responded to each other, then, and subsequently.

Paul recovered enough to be distracted by an ice cream and he was soon quite magnanimous with John. As they became pals again, Ann went into a mood!

It was just a few days after this that Paul had come to the room and asked if he could have a den that would be his alone. He was a very small boy so the place under the small table was just fine.

When he entered the room on the day of the incident he looked as if he wanted to give somebody a good kick and a long bite. And, in keeping with previous episodes, he was coming straight in my direction. I had to hold him because he was ready to break anything in sight and this included me. He needed and wanted to be held.

It was one of those experiences when you end up on the floor, or partly jammed under a chair, while you are reassuring the child that you understand that they have a lot of very angry feelings – and that that's all right; that you can take that; that you aren't going to let them hurt or damage you; or hurt or damage themselves; that you are going to hold them and stay with them – while at the same time you are encouraging them to try to tell you what exactly it is that has made them feel so angry.

After about five minutes, as Paul began using words to express his anger, the writhing and kicking became a little less fierce. At the peak of it, however, he decided to take a bite out of my arm. As I felt his teeth against the skin I was able to prevent them from going too far in. It was at this point I conveniently remembered that there was one apple left in the tray on the cupboard.

While all this was happening there had been one other boy in the room. He had known me long enough to understand what I was doing and he had been quietly proceeding to make a tray very close to where the apple was. I called out to him to please get it from the tray and bring it to me. He very quickly found it then came over and waited until I could safely get a hand free. He gave me the apple. I apologised for only having one. He said that was OK and returned to his sand tray to continue working on it.

As the next attempt was made to take a bite of me, I placed the apple in front of Paul's teeth and they accepted it. A few minutes later, while he was in the process of eating the apple, I had easily hauled him onto an armchair beside me. Both of us were well supported by the seat.

I was at the back of it and he was in front of me between my knees. We were both facing outwards. With one of my arms I was holding him around the waist. With the other I held the apple as he ate it. When we had talked about why he was so angry I let go of the the apple completely. He took hold of it. I then put both arms round him and held him a bit more firmly.

He began to relax beside me. Just sitting there he ate the apple.

When he had finished it he said quietly that he thought he would make a tray. This consisted of some small plastic aeroplanes set out in a very ordered formation. There were no biting and devouring creatures in sight. It should be stressed that he had only rarely produced a tray in which something did not have its teeth dug into something else.

He then said 'cheerio' and informed me that he was going downstairs to his class.

I knew something important had happened and wanted to tell someone about it, but this isn't the kind of story that can easily be told, and anyway there wasn't anyone around at the time who would have wanted to hear it.

The other boy got his apple the following day.

Part IV

Into Deeper Territory

The intention here is to present some of the words and images which were produced in and around the sand trays and at Talk and Draw, as a means of illustrating the materials in action. Also, by straying slightly from this agenda into the supplementary notes which were recorded at the time of the visit, it should be possible to bed down what the children had to say into a wider plot.

Some of the stories belong to children who have already been introduced, but there are some new arrivals on the scene. Wherever possible, how they or their productions relate to anything which has gone before or is still to come will be remarked upon.

The words which were spoken by the children have been kept as intact as possible. Minor changes of a predominantly grammatical kind have been made only where it was felt they might assist comprehension.

I would like to make two observations of a more general kind. Not only in these stories but in all those which were reappraised in preparation for this part of the book, I was forcibly struck by the extent to which death and sexual abuse dominated the children's concerns. And there is a matter which raises some interesting questions about therapeutic practice and what kind of relationship is of most value to the child: it was remarkable how frequently a brief contact with a child outside the unit brought with it a pivotal shift in the quality of our relationship, and a subsequent improvement in my capacity to be of help.

23

EXAMPLES OF TALK AND DRAW

The words which are written down during Talk and Draw rarely give a complete and accurate account of what is said. The spelling is often inaccurate, words are repeated by mistake, there is very little punctuation and sometimes, in the rush to record as much as possible of the child's contribution, the worker's interventions are limited to a question mark. At the time these examples were produced I was obviously more interested in what the children had to say than in anything I wanted to ask.[19] And, as I had no intention of using them in a book when they were produced (a factor which might well have influenced their content), they provide a relatively reliable picture of the procedure in practice. This also applies to the tray stories.

MORE THAN A SCRAWL

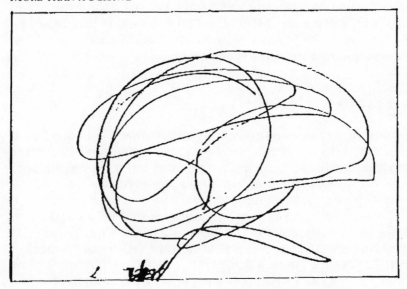

7 years 1 months

---

[19] Words of mine which were recorded at the time of the production are given in italics to differentiate them from those of the children.

The first example has been included for two reasons. It has a value for the child which can be easily overlooked and, with no accompanying words, a fact which should perhaps disqualify it from inclusion, it represents one end of the range of what is produced at Talk and Draw.

On several occasions a sequence of drawings, each very similar to the one presented, was produced as a prelude to a stark admission of some troubling incident. During one of these a boy, reaching the fourteenth drawing of a series of twenty-one, told me he had killed a bird with a golf stick. Doing the fifteenth he said a lady had been watching him from a car.

Concern for the paper supplies had sometimes led me to intrude on this process but, if the child appeared to be well focused on the task, experience had taught that it was worth staying the course until completion.

The boy who produced this picture had a penchant for surreptitiously provoking bigger boys into making a physical attack on him, before leaping swiftly into the arms of a sympathetic worker for protection. Several of his drawings suggested he had been involved in sexual activity of a kind which was causing him a great deal of upset. He increasingly improved his ability to pack things away and settle to the demands of school. Whether or not, in the long term, this proved to be in his best interests, I neither knew him well enough nor long enough to comment.

WARMING UP WITH WORDS

In contrast, in this second example I believe that words rather than lines were being used as a warm-up to the expression of a specific incident. On this occasion it is not revealed, but seven months later the rocket motif in the centre of the picture was drawn again during a disclosure of sexual abuse.

This was probably the longest 'story' ever told at Talk and Draw. It was a masterpiece for the boy concerned who, during his preceding seven visits, had produced some rather stark images of such features as a house, a figure and a television set. It may well be that he lost sight of what he wanted to say in the delight of seeing so many of his words displayed on the paper before him.

No one had been in any doubt that this boy's life at home and out of school was chaotic, but it was with this story that he began to indicate it himself.

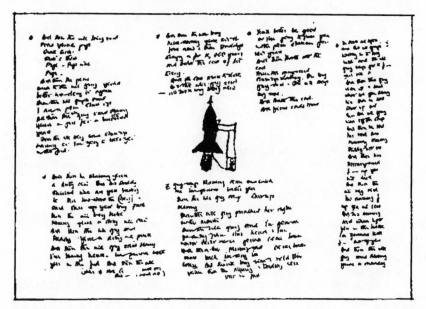

9 years

The doors are open and this wee guys walking in to say hello and the wee guy says get to f— you wee a –

And then this guy come up and said what are you doing here then he said shut up and then the wee guy went off the ship

And then he told his told his Mummy Mummy Daddy hit me

And then Mummy said f— up you wee dick

And then the wee boy told his mummy f up you we(e) cow

And his Mummy said when I get you in the hoose I'm gonnae kick f— out of you

And then the wee guy said Mummy you're a monkey

And then he Mammy you're a dirty cow Then his Daddy shouted who are you talking to then the(boy) said shut up you big prick

Then the wee boy hello Mummy you're a dirty wee cow

And then the wee guy said Daddy you're a dirty wee prick

And then the wee guy said Mammy I'm leaving house. I'm going to boot you in the fud. and then the wee *he asks if Mrs P. the head teacher will see this – I say no*

And then the wee guy says Mammy come on and catch me I'm gonnae batter you

Then the wee guy says shut up Mammy

Then the wee guy punched her right on the mouth

Then the wee guy said I'm gonnae go away from this house and I'm never gonna come back come back I'm sorry I'm sorry.

And then the wee boy went and told the polis then Mummy and Daddy were put in jail.

And then the wee boy said

Polis you're pigs

Oink oink

Who's there

Pigs — pigs who

Pigs —

And then the polis said to the wee guy you'd better no do it again

Then the wee guy said I am a police shut up

And then the wee guy said Mammy you're in jail for a hundred 100 years

Then the wee boy said shut up Mammy or I'm going to boot you in the fud.

And then the wee boy hello Mummy you're out of jail now and then Daddy's staying in for 10,000 years and that's the end of the story.

And it's still mair to dae

And the wee guy said – no he's a big boy now

You'd better be good or I'm going to put you in the polis station for 100 years

And then that's not the end

Then the guy said shut up Mammy. The big guy said the wee boys big now.

And that's the end.

And your end's meet.

Incidentally the boy who told this story had an unusually vague attitude towards tray-making. He was not averse to it, it just seemed rather incidental to him compared to some of his other pursuits. He was, for example, extremely fond of bobos and it was for these, and the possibility of meeting up with a boy who had interests similar to his own, that he began to make more frequent visits to the room. (His associate will be introduced in the tray stories as the boy who made a brand new bridge.)

That mutual 'interest' is reflected quite succinctly in the following list of what he declared were some of his more recent acquisitions. It has been taken straight from a Talk and Draw 'picture' and from under the heading 'I Stole'.

There is no indication in the words recorded that we jointly agreed to number the items and the original list did not have capital letters.

1   Mars Bars
2   Twixies
3   Chewing gum, 4 packets.

4   Ginger[20]
5   Loaf of bread
6   4 bottles of ginger for me and my pals
7   Biscuits
8   Crisps
9   Wee dummy guns
10   Toys
11   Jigsaws
12   Tapes
13   Radio set
14   Some scissor (*he said word without an 's' at the end*)

The next drawing is also by him. It has been chosen mainly as a good illustration of a child's capacity, when ready, to give a very detailed account of what might be troubling them. And with this example only, I am including some background information to the incident depicted. This will allow me to address an issue which was germane to understanding of both his other stories and those of many of the other children.

THE MAN IN THE PARK

It was only four months after the rocket picture had been that before I recorded anything else of his at Talk and Draw. When I did, the details of an experience which had been initiated in a park began to unfold. This unfolding occurred over a three-month period until I was the recipient of a vivid but rather fractured tale of an encounter he had had with a man who had given him money to perform certain sexual acts.

Following on from this, and in line with statutory requirements on receiving a disclosure of sexual abuse, he and I shared the story with his own social worker. What happened next was totally out of our control as arrangements were made for him to be interviewed by another social worker in a different setting, and then by a police woman and a police surgeon in a different place again.

Excruciated, but willing throughout, he was not believed by either the police woman or the police surgeon and their response influenced his own social worker into taking the same view.

---

[20] A local name for lemonade.

This was a dreadful experience in many respects but not one to expand on here. What can be said in its favour is that we got to know each other much better, over the several hours spent waiting to be 'seen', and the quality of our contact improved immeasurably. Again, in praise of outside experiences, I believe it was instrumental to his producing, about thirty days later, a full account of the previously fragmented tale. The fragmentation may well have influenced his interviewers into thinking he had made it all up; although why they thought he might have done so is beyond comprehension.

The words on the drawing were interspersed with the names of the people and places which featured in the incident. These have been deleted and I am presenting only a summary of the information he provided.

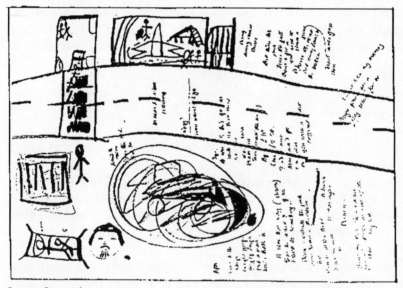

9 years 8 months

He had been with a friend when the incident took place. He told me the name and address of the other boy involved. He described the area of the park where they had met the man, the gate and the fence which needed to be climbed to get into the park when it was closed, and he drew the face and features of the man who had given them the money.

After meeting in the park they had gone to a house. He was able to describe the bed on which his friend had been abused and the carpet in the room. He changed the story several times about the amount of money they had been given but his account of what they purchased after receiving it remained constant. He and his pal had gone to the shops and bought ginger and a bag of chips.

Several weeks after our visit to the police, it became known that sexual attacks on young boys had been occurring in similar circumstances and in the same area of the park which he had described.

And now the issue to which I was referring earlier.

During that first six months, almost all the drawings he produced had contained features of penises in various guises; these had been given names like a lightbulb, a nose and an aeroplane. As the number of disclosures of sexual abuse increased, it was observed that children frequently changed the names and characteristics of persons, objects and places associated with the experience, as a means of disguising and distancing themselves from it. It was as if by doing this they were creating a kind of half-way stage towards disclosure, and one from which they could retreat back into safety, if the response of the person receiving the information did not measure up to what was needed. How this process manifests itself in the children's work is illustrated in the material I have chosen to conclude the sample of tray stories.

What follows here is a Talk and Draw example (without the picture) of how it was employed in one of his stories.

> This little boy [was] walking down the road and then he got bit by a dog and then the dog peed in his face then the dog done a shite in his face. Then that's it then.

In his discussion with the police woman and the surgeon he had described the green stuff which had come from the man, asking them after he had done so for reassurance that he would not have contracted some sort of disease.

Drawing Out Anger with Words

The girl in 'Three Reluctances' who was frightened of being thought of as bad did a lot of drawings like this next example. I am unable to use any of those she produced as each one included the names of the people who were the focus of her anger or upset.

This one has been chosen mainly because it is free of names. It was also done by a girl but it was a form of expression common to both boys and girls.

9 years 10 months

A Message

Objects were often 'left' lying around the room as children moved from one medium of expression to another. Some were undoubtedly messages and I probably missed many of them in the rush. Whilst they offered a feast of interpretive opportunities, there was no need for conjecture about this one. It was not produced in my presence but was left for me to find. When I failed to do this as quickly as the girl would have liked, she directed me to it, from a distance.

It was a detail from another chain of sexual incidents and these were imparted to me in a variety of ways. I was talked to directly, I had information passed on to me by another girl and on one occasion was given a detailed description of her worst experience from behind a thick piece of cardboard. She was in one of the hiding places in the room while I sat on the floor outside it writing down what she said.

9 years 10 months

As indicated in the introduction to this section, the issue of sexual abuse was rarely off the agenda once the room was well established. The extent to which it was affecting so many of the children's lives was, for a long time, almost beyond belief. The evidence however became irrefutable and its incidence in the work is reflected in the examples of Talk and Draw and in the tray stories.

To place the girl who produced this example: she is the one who developed a liking for milk in a bottle after being unwilling to take one as a baby. A notable aspect of her behaviour was a profound lack of trust and with her I underwent a more prolonged testing-out than I did with any of the other children. And that includes David. She was not as wild as he had been but she was more unremittingly persistent.

The words on the drawing which I added after it was completed are 'Drawn while I was elsewhere in the room.'

THE LOST DOGS

The same girl produced the next picture of dogs within dogs. I was referring to the dogs she had lost when I listed, much earlier in the text, the range of concerns which had emerged at the procedure of Talk and Draw.

Her lack of trust in adults had no doubt been contributed to by her mother, whose attitude to the many dogs she had loved and lost was at the very least ambivalent. The girl could recall in vivid detail an occasion when her mother had lied about one of the them and taken it to the vet's to be put to sleep while she was at school. She had run away from home that day. Dogs were important to a lot of the children and it seems only right that they should make an appearance here.

9 years 10 months

The dog which was put to sleep is in the picture, along with one that got knocked down and one that had run away. The smallest dog was probably still alive. She spoke of wanting a basket for it. In the drawing their very distinctive names were intertwined with a description of their fates. I have chosen to delete all the words, leaving the dogs to have their unadulterated day.

The Stolen Toy Helicopter

The next two stories are of single events and were told by the same boy.

He was a child who seemed to be in a constant state of anxiety, as if expecting something to jump out at him at any moment. The shock he said he had experienced when he got caught stealing was completely understandable. His nervousness became even more comprehensible when, just days before he was about to move on to

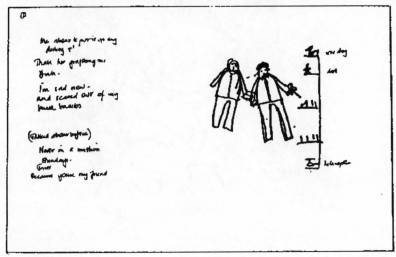

9 years 11 months

secondary school, he told me about all the times in his life he had been hit. This had occurred both within his own family and during a foster placement.

'Me about to put it up my dukey.
That's her grabbing me. Huh.
I'm sad now – and scared out of my knick knocks.'
?Talked about before
'Never in a million Sundays.
Trust
Because you're my friend.'

NO BREAKFAST

This is the picture which was referred to in the chapter 'From No Breast to No Breakfast'.

9 years 10 months

'He didnae give me any breakfast this morning because he shited his pants and he didnae have enough time.'

GETTING A JAG

The boy who did the following two pictures had haemophilia. In the first example, and for the first time, he begins to tell me how he really feels about getting his Factor 8 injections and about his many visits to hospital.

'I've got something bothering me.
I had to go to hospital today for a check up because of my ankle. It's sore. I'm building a big tray. Gie me a jag. That's all.'

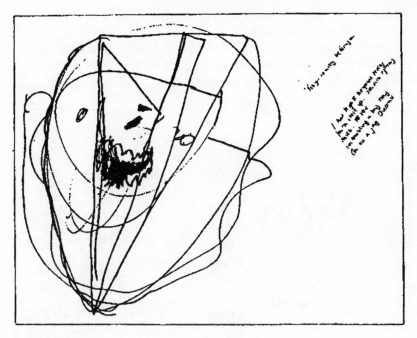

8 years 8 months

STOPPING PLAYING THE CLOWN

This picture was drawn three months later. He began to make regular visits to the room and had ceased putting on an act of being pleasantly cheeky and happy. His parents were separated and he told me how angry he got when they argued about who he should be living with.

It is interesting to relate yet again that it was probably as a result of a trip outside the unit that a significant shift was made in our understanding of each other. My perception of him had until then been influenced by others' descriptions of how he behaved in the outside world. All I had observed on his visits to the room was a bright faced, active boy who was delighted to be making trays. On the trip to which I am referring he was reticent about going into a café, extremely anxious once inside, and in need of constant reassurance about when and where we would be going afterwards.

He was a boy who had missed a lot of school but, based on the way he functioned in the room, I became totally convinced that he would have responded well to continuing his education in a mainstream primary school.

He was another of the children I failed badly in that I was unable to persuade those responsible for making such decisions that such a move would be in his best interests.

8 years 8 months

Said he wanted to draw at the desk.

'It's a house. It's a man's house, there's trees and cars and a mammy and a wee boy. The boy says fuck off to his Mammy and the Daddy says fuck off you wee bastard I'll put you in jail. There's the wee boy dressed up as a wee clown. There's the wee boy putting his Da's tire [tyre] down because he was fighting with him.

The wee [boy] ran in the door and smashed the windows. Then all the door fell down. All the windows are smashed. He made a big hole in the roof. He's nine. He put all his Da's bricks lined up at the wall, there's his Dad's tools, he threw them out the window and he jumped through the roof and he made another hole. Then he says fuck off my cow I'm going to put you in jail. There's the wee boy now, he's a policeman now and he says to his Daddy if you don't start behaving yoursell I'll put you in jail for a 100 years. The wee boy says fuck off Dad I'm going to put you in jail. And his Mammy stayed for 100 years then he got her back out. And that's the end of the story.'

Bad Dreams

Bad dreams have been requesting a mention since I began writing up the work. It is not that I have anything substantial to say about the subject. Indeed with dreams similar to the ones I am about to present here, I adopted a rather simplistic response. Whether or not I would react to them in the same way now is difficult to assess.

The two examples which I have chosen are both of dreams which occurred after a child had gone to bed feeling extremely angry with a sibling. My suggestion to the child that there might be a connection between the anger and the dream was usually acknowledged with ease. We would then follow that up with a discussion of strategies for managing the relationship better in future.

I kept no records of this but should have done, as there were numerous occasions on which this kind of intervention proved helpful in preventing a recurrence of the dream.

In the first example an anticipated retaliation has attached itself to a creature from a horror movie or video. This happened frequently.

Freddie Kruger

'Bad dreams when I was wee.

He's a big scary monster and do you know where he was do you know where he lives – in the Clyde.

He nearly went and tore down a cable ma Dad told me.

He is real. He went and pulled down a big building. Ma Da showed me the bricks. I saw him and I had to run away.'

? Not getting mixed up.

'It's been happening for the last couple of days.' *[being angry].*

? 'Angry with ma brother. Thousands. Since I've been at my old school. If some ...'

Feels like he'd really like to hurt somebody.

'Just punch and kill someone.'

Big angry feelings.

'Freddie Kruger

There's his claws one two three four five.

He's got these gloves on it then he kills people with the claws.
Dreamt it thousands of times.
Video. In my hoose. In the dream.
He went and scratched me on the back and scratched me on the face and on the front.'

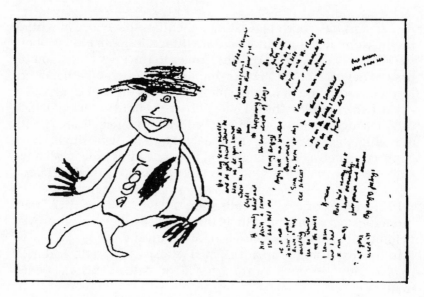

8 years 1 months

BUGS UNDER THE STAIRS

All things that are bothering.
'Wee sisters not well – a bug that flies about in the air
Want my wee sister to get well
Ma big brother jumps on my racer when I'm at school – sometimes he goes away and doesn't come back
Dreaming about this
I'm dreaming about that again
I cannae come down these stairs I don't like it cos I don't like that
I feel there's stuff coming out of it wee monsters.' *he draws one.*
'Wee bones you can see his on telly, he's only got down to his knees.'
? how many times – 'five or six times all holiday
I never had one last ...
I think I know what keeps them away.'
dreams

'I feel like punching his head and slinging his hi-fi out the window.
Punch his heed in. That's all then make him no go on my bike.
It's a picture of ma hoose.' 'W' [*the boy's first initial*] coming down the
stairs.
'That's the cupboard. It's got shoes in it.'

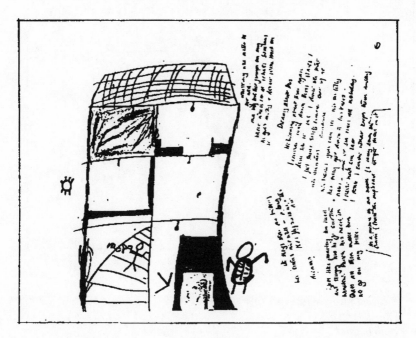

11 years 10 months

Bad dreams also feature in this following series of four drawings
which were produced by the boy whose lunchtime visit to talk about
the death of his grandfather was given an airing in the opening
chapters.[21]

Although tending to the loss of his grandfather was the foremost
issue, he also brought into our discussion the anger he felt towards
big boys in his street who were being unkind to him. This was a
matter which we took up on a later occasion.

The titles of the examples are based simply on their content.

---

[21] Most of the boy's words which were quoted then came from the example entitled
'Worries'. They have been repeated here for ease of reference.

GOD'S CHAIR

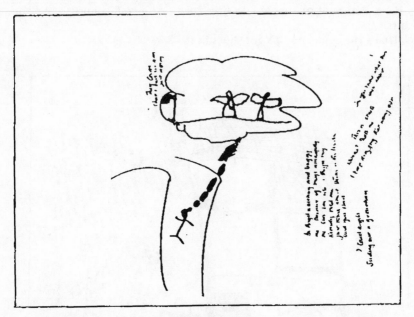

9 years 5 months

'Do you know what this one's about.
This is streets.'
Who is this?
'That's me, I keep dragging this worry out
That's God's chair and that's his arm just sitting
Good angels sending out a guardian
? An angel watching and bugging me
Because of boys annoying me. Cos I'm wee they're big
Nobody told me
Just think about them in the house and you start.'

THE GRANDFATHER

? 'To the graveyard – stayed there for ever
Buying a big truck
Tickled me (try to smile)
Always wanted you to come and see.'
Always in your grandfather's house. 'Grandfather OLD nice

He died
Just greeted for him in my bed. (Nobody else cried.)'

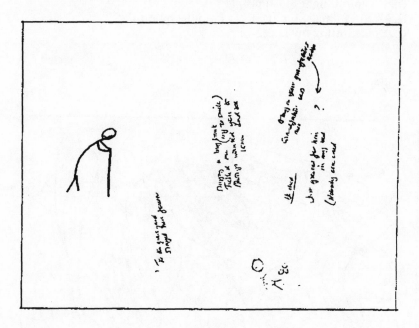

FOXES AND WHALES

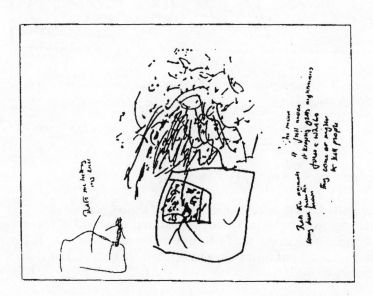

? 'The moon. It full moon.
It keeping getting nightmares foxes and whales
They come at night to kill people.
That's the animals coming down from the moon
That's me hitting my knee.'

WORRIES

    Had left to make a tray then said he'd another teeny weeny worry and came back to desk to draw again.
    'teeny weeny worry
    This is all my worries I'm getting out. I'm covering the page. That's it.'

THE BIGGEST DINOSAUR IN THE WORLD

The boy who did the sequence of drawings above also did this one nine days before. The room was being painted and most of the toys were in the store cupboard. I can not be certain now that it was entirely his idea to draw a tray, rather than make one, but that is my memory of it.

This was the only 'tray' which was ever 'drawn'. It has been included for that reason and because it represents one of the many drawings in which something was eating or getting eaten.

9 years 8 months

'This is the big tray.
The biggest dinosaur in the world.
This is the blood. It's been eating human beings.
That's the big tongue
That's the human beings
That's the big body.
Do you know what this is. Its an upside down bat having to sleep having nightmares
? Big horrid monster coming to eat Miss [*my name deleted*]. That's it shouting for help.
It's written terrible – upside down.
There's me getting a big arm touching the sand real sand [*in the tray at the side of drawing*] covered the monsters face in it and that's it.'

THE MONSTER

Another example with a similar theme. It is one of several done by
a boy who, for reasons which will be evident in a moment, is referred
to as Tom of the Bumblebees. He is also one of the main contribu-
tors to the tray stories.

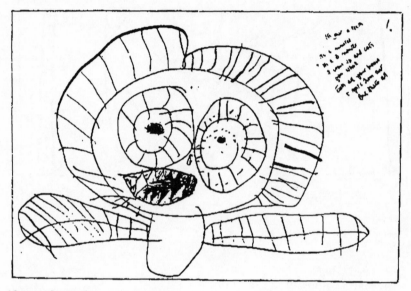

12 years 8 months

'It's just got teeth. It's a monster
It comes up and eats you whole
Eats all your bones and spits them out. And that's all.'

ESCAPE FROM A WATER BOX (1)

The main subject of this Talk and Draw also featured in a sand tray
which was constructed on the same visit. How it featured is described
in the tray stories under the same heading.

Always tell
? 'My cousin Jean – she pisses the bed
She doesn't dae it as mair as I dae it

Wee James – he does it in Auntie Mary's bed because he gets a bottle with hundred of milk in it.'

? Feelings

'You say oh not again

I feel that I hate myself now

I'm dead scared and I don't like it.

I don't know how I f- piss the bed.'

? when

'Na. Staying with Aunt Margaret

If I pissed the bed I got a doing – with a slipper head hand feet – put to bed for a month straight when I came home from school

Da's. Never really done it there.'

? Why

'I still don't really do it in Aunt Mary's

Comes some nights and comes back. I just hide it and run away

Make my bed. ? Sometimes she checks

She gies me a slap and sends me to bed cos I never told her. And then it smells – '

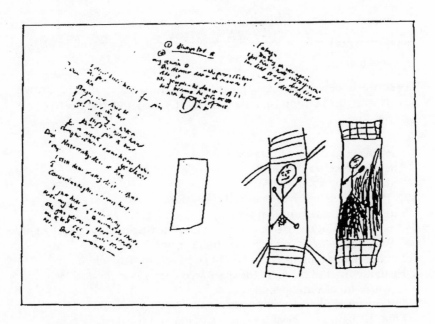

10 years 4 months

GRIEVING FOR THE MOTHER

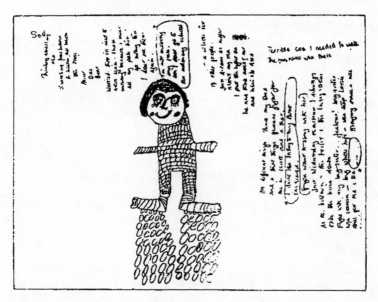

10 years 4 months

Three days before the escape picture, the same boy had drawn another around which he talked about his life since the death of his mother.

'Terrible cos I needed to walk
The bus never was there.
Sad. Thinking about my Ma
Switching frae hoose to hoose all the time
Aunt Mary. Da's. Aunt Margaret
Worried that I'll need to move again I hate moving because I meet all my pals then I go away then I don't see them again
I'm not making any pals cos I don't go to an ordinary school.'
He names four of his pals. *They have been deleted from the drawing.*
'A whole lot of other people
Just dream at night about my ma.
I put the light on – lie and think aboot her and she died.
All different things. Think my Dad and a' that they're gonnae fight for me in court and a' that
I don't like talking to my Aunt Mary. I'm scared.'

If you want to stay with her
'Just Wednesday sometime I always do the kitchen and the toilet and the living room take the bins down.

Fight with my big sister. Jealous ? big sister wee cousin – big whole hi-fi – wee step lassie still got Ma Da. Jean staying since [she was] a wee lassie.'

This boy had an excellent relationship with his class teacher and, although the culture of the room was undoubtedly of some assistance in freeing him up to talk more easily about his grief and the bed-wetting, she did the follow-up work on both these issues.

DEATH OF A CHILD

There were very strong feelings of guilt and regret as this story was told and the girl recalled her mother's reproaches for not having rescued the baby.

It was just one of the many awful things that had happened to her throughout her life. The behaviour of some of the adults she had known, particularly towards children and animals, verged on the horrific. She was the child who had told me in a state of extreme anxiety that her mother's cheekbone was bruised. It was only later that I understood what was fuelling the distress. She explained how frightened she had been that the bone might come bursting through her face at any moment.

In the transcript there is a sentence about something 'I'd seen' the previous day and this requires some explanation. The bus attendant from the unit had been unavailable to make the journey home with the children and I had travelled with them. This was the only time I had ever gone on this particular route. The girl now assumed I had a detailed knowledge of the area where she lived and that I would recognise her description of exactly where the accident had taken place. The 'big thingby' she refers to is a pigeon loft.

And once again the contact on the bus, outside the unit, may well have precipitated the telling of this story the following day.

'Scared
When the light goes out in ma room and even the hall light. And even the lobby light
And …
A wee baby. It got stuck in one [of] they wee birdy things that get painted green and the birdies sit inside it
It fell in and died

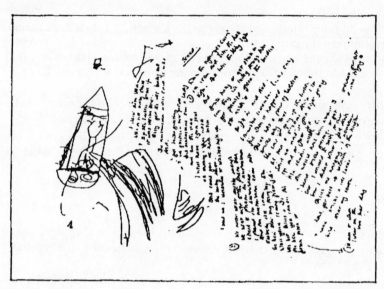

11 years 4 months

I can still remember I was only five when it happened.

There was a pair of ladders.

It was only three.

We saw it going up the ladder and we told it to come down and it said no and it just kept going up and it just fell

Ma Cousin [The name was given; it has been deleted]

She would have been about 3

? Heard. It was greeting. It got out – it didn't get out – it was trying to I wanted to take it out but I didn't want to fall down.

There's me hanging – I wouldn't have got back up because of the height. It was a wee lassie lived near my cousin.

We never went quickly enough

We went over to the phone box

And tried to phone an ambulance and phoned an ambulance.

And an ambulance came out. Nobody else came.

See how that big thingby – she –

When you're coming from K. L.'s wee bit

How you can see the fitba' pitch'

! had seen it when I travelled on the bus that day.

'I don't told them there was a wee baby stuck

? Up the ladder to see if it was down there.

They got the wee baby out

The ambulance man said it was deed.

? feel

I was greeting
? No grown [ups] two people
Two ambulance, one a lady
And one the man
I went hame. I just told ma mammy and that was it.
[Her mother had asked] How could you no have taken the baby down.
I said I couldnae it was too high up.'

SENDING A MESSAGE UP TO SPACE

The response to the symbolic, when it made an appearance at Talk and Draw, was much the same as when it appeared in the tray constructions, it was rarely addressed directly. There were usually plenty of other issues to be focused on; ones which were being communicated verbally. As already indicated, many of those initially expressed in symbolic form receded from view to reappear at a later date as conscious concerns.

The next drawing was done by a boy who was reluctant to make any marks on paper with pens, pencils or paint. Once we had established a workable level of trust, the role I took up with him was more interventionist than it had been with any other child. He was probably the most defended boy with whom I had worked. The first time he tried painting I actually held his hand lightly as he put the brush into the paint and transferred it to the paper.

In the situation in which this picture was produced I was using Talk and Draw to try to warm him up a little. He drew a lot after this and began to enjoy it, even touching through his drawings on the very tender feelings he had for his father, who had left home when he was a baby. I think he did get some relief from this but there were far too many pressures on him for me to risk more than a little encouragement to open up. His father had been been declared a villain by all the main players in his immediate and extended family and any expression of such feelings would have been totally unacceptable to them.

There is more about his use of the room in the series of stories entitled 'Sausage Egg and Beans Four Times'.

11 years 6 months

'Draw anything
It's an alien sending a message up to space. And its a full moon.
And the moon's dead bright
The guy's plukey
He's got bags under his eyes
There's a bat. [drawn]
And there's the grass
And there's another bat a bigger one this time
It's a chinkey bat
It's got big teeth and the other ones got wee teeth. And the wee one's got hair. But the big ones got hair on his side of his head but he's got one wee teeny hat on the top of his head and it's like a Y And there's a cloud. The winds blowing and there's two hurricanes.
    That's it.'

TOM OF THE BUMBLEBEES

In the next picture a boy called Tom has depicted himself and his three brothers as bumblebees. Tom is the figure on the far right.

Douglas, a brother who attracted most of Tom's negative attentions, is second from the left and Gordon, for whom his feelings were usually quite tender, is over on the far left. The smallest figure is the baby.[22]

12 years 8 months

'Well that's me.
They're bumble bees.
That's a'.
They're flying.'
? do you want to do more
'No I'm going to come in every day and do one fucking picture.'

Tom was the boy whose interest in the imitation feeding bottle led to the employment of a real one. How this came about is covered in the tray stories. Meanwhile these two examples of Talk and Draw should help to set the scene. This has been a serious business so far and the first drawing, which has a certain humorous quality about it, has been chosen partly to provide some light relief.

---

[22] On this occasion only, I cropped the picture to give the bumblebees full exposure.

His brothers were drawn as bumblebees to illustrate the behaviour of the four boys in the family as they sought their mother's attention in the morning. The second example, about the lost socks, will allow me to make further comment about the usefulness of Talk and Draw as a medium around which the children could address everyday concerns; accepting at the same time that some of these had much deeper implications and that both needed to be tackled in tandem.

THE LOST SOCKS

This was produced on 5 November, hence the use of fireworks to portray the anticipated ructions when he got home. Much of the distress which he brought in to school each day stemmed from the state of his relationship with his mother as he left the house each morning.

The issue of the lost socks provided an opportunity to talk about the demands of the four children on their mother. It led to an ongoing discussion of the feelings of jealousy he had for his brothers. We did air the possibility that he was losing his socks every morning as a means of focusing her attention on him, a notion which provoked much delight.

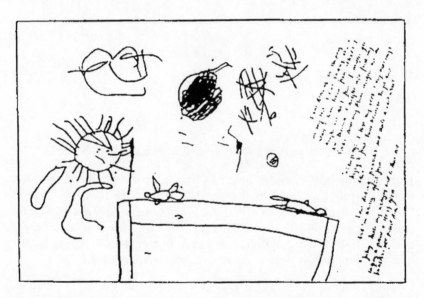

12 years 8 months

'I am drawing me sleeping in my bed. I was thinking about when I come home from school I might not have fun. I might get hit because I might not find my socks and my Mum might hit me.

Two days ago. I lost my sock and my Mammy's trying to find them because they're new ones.

I am drawing fireworks and that's a cartwheel and I'm having good fun.'

? feeling

'That's my worrying and a' that out. I'm going to paint a lot of good fireworks – not paint, draw.'

The effectiveness of the work in the room would have been considered unsatisfactory if it had not included, in substantial measure, the development of common-sense strategies for dealing with the children's everyday difficulties inside and outside the unit. At the end of our time together this boy's overwhelming concern had become his relationship with his girlfriend. He still behaved very much like a bumblebee but through the plans we had devised he was in much better control of his socks.

24

A SAMPLE OF TRAY STORIES[23]

It seems appropriate to begin with some of David's stories, and the first was told about three months after he joined my group. It belongs with the tray in which he was tending to a woman doll. It is followed by a series of four others which he told over the course of two days, three weeks later.

Several of the phrases which were used in Part Two to illustrate his constructive intentions were extracted from these stories.

David has put a blue-and-white striped bowl in the centre left of the big tray. He stands on it to make a mound then begins to jump on it quite forcefully. He follows this by turning it over. Gradually he becomes more intense and involved.

'It's a big land and they're all going to have a big show and they're all going to see a big tonka truck jumping over a big burn, a big pool.'

The bowl is half-filled with water. David decides to put some people in the tray; there have been none before. He places a plastic woman doll into the pool. He is making little noises as he does so, 'huh huh huh', odd wee noises; he is very preoccupied. The doll is placed face down.

David goes to get an empty, miniature packet of bandages. He opens it up, pulls bits off and tries to make it into a cover for the woman's body. It doesn't fit as he would like it to and he throws it away. He then gets silver paper and wraps this around her middle. He is singing to himself and making more noises. David then takes her out of the pool and tries to put her on a ladder which has been leaned against its side. She won't stay there so he stands her up in the sand at the side of it. I ask what she is doing.

'Look, haud on.'

Smiling quite gently he shows the doll to another boy in the room who acknowledges her nakedness. Now the silver paper has been taken off. It is placed at the top of the ladder beside a small man figure.

'It's a towel. She gets out and gets a towel from the wee man. She had to get out because the truck was ready to get revved up. She fell back in when

---

[23] The questions which appear in the tray stories are a legacy from a time of unwarranted intrusions, before the decision had been made to let the children's tray-work proceed unhindered. A strong temptation to delete some of them has been resisted and each one has been kept scrupulously in place.

she went to get out because the edge was dead slippy. Then she got out and stood by her house. One of the wee owners who got this set up, he was telling the driver when he was ready and then he ran and fell over.

Haud on.

Where's all the rulers.[24] And he thought everything was all going to turn out and he went up the ramp. Something happened to the tyre and thingby. He sat waiting for the guy to tell him to go. He must have done something to his back wheel and he fell in. [The truck goes into the pool.]

And it didn't turn out right.'

I ask if there is anything else.

'And he said maybe next time I'll be able to do it or I'll get luck. And that's his wee garage over there.'

The sand in the tray is damp and flattened down. The truck referred to is a small red and white plastic one with black wheels and, apart from the people who are standing around to observe the action, there are some fences, two pine-cones and a tree. Two small horses stand side by side in the bottom right corner of the tray. The ramp is more of a bridge. It spans the gap between the right-side edge of the sand tray and the rim of the bowl.

The notes which accompany the next three stories suggest that his mood, when they were told, was influenced by his having sorted out some of the things which had been troubling him. I am presenting them in full.

David looked perturbed this morning. Eventually he said his brother had kept him awake with stories of rats in the room. He said he had been watching a horror film where a greedy baby-sitter had suddenly had her throat cut. He was 'easier' after acknowledging this had been upsetting for him. He said he had been awake until two a.m.

Cups had been broken in class last week and David had been responsible. The subject resurfaced when we tried to find cups for hot chocolate.

He got upset again but did remarkably well, admitting to having 'done it' and later apologising to one of the boys whose cup had been included in the breakages.

Noticing a look of satisfaction on his face at having confronted and resolved a difficulty, I commented on how well he was doing. This was the prelude to making three trays which he referred to as episodes one, two and three.[25]

---

[24] Measuring rulers were popular and mostly used to improvise bridges.

[25] Children in my group frequently made trays which consisted of parts or episodes. It was a practice which was copied by children visiting from other groups, but one which seemed to fade away once the room was established for the use of everyone in the unit. I suspected for a while that it was being used as a ploy to retain possession of the big tray, as this was the most coveted and the one around which it most often occurred.

They were all produced in the big tray using very damp sand. To start with, the main objects and characters were a green plastic boat, an orange bowl, some green metal fences, some yellow wooden ones, three pebbles, three houses, three trees, several very small figures and a monkey. As the stories unfold, other objects and creatures make an appearance.

David said:

'I'm going to make trays all day.

Episode one.

This is what it was like at [name of a seaside town] when we went.

They're having a bit of bother getting the boat out because it's been raining overnight and its soaked all the sand up and its gone all into the boat and the little monkey's laughing away at himself.

And the way they've got it out the wee bottom bit under the boat has got stuck on a rock and they cannae get it out.

See the policeman up at the tree, he was there because there's been a break-in and he was watching to see if anybody else came.

Then they got the ladders and tried to get up to the wee monkey's house and the wee monkey started screaming and the little gorilla heard him and the crocodile.'

David took a plastic baby doll from the trays of toys, held it, then put it back and picked up a small wooden figure.

'The robbers killed one of the wee babies and there he is.

David puts him in the boat which is partly filled with water, then moves him to the end of the boat beside some other small figures.

'And the grandpa and the Dad and everybody is watching the boat to see if it gets moved.

Dad's shouting and swearing. He's in a bad mood and says he can't move the boat himself. Come and help, he says to the others.

Then Grandpa goes down and helps him and they manage to get it moved a wee bit but they're going to have to dig out the tree [this is in a small mound near the boat] so they can get it away. That's it.

In the next one the boat's gonna – be out here, it gets moved.

This one's got three episodes in it.'

David is singing as he proceeds. He has emptied the water out of the boat and is mixing it in with the sand.

In Episode Two he puts the wee tree in a tub of real soil then gets three pebbles from the shelf. He'd brought them in that morning.

'They managed to get the boat moved and the policeman seen a robber going in to one of the flats.

And the way he started his bike his front wheel hit the fence and he tumbled over and fell into the next park and all the wee children ran over to see if he was alright.

The wee monkey heard the noise and came and started laughing.

And episode three, the third one, will look brilliant.

[?] The alligator's sunbathing and he's dead angry because the gorilla won't let him into the pool.

[?] The gorilla wants everything to himself and that's it.'

'Episode three.

The trees starting to grow everywhere now and all the fences are coming away. And they're coming to this end now and to make this end safe and to make this end look nicer and better.

And I'll be putting this boat in here.

Look Miss this end is looking nice.

He's got a serious injury but he'll have to ride the bike. He's just sitting there again to see if anything else happens.'

David washes the motor bike in the pool and washes the 'wee' people as he moves them around. He is singing 'When the Saints Go Marching In' as he changes the formation of the sand.

'All the neighbours are complaining because they see all the workers making this end all nice.

That's them growing all the trees now, it's autumn, no, what's that time when everything starts growing [*I suggest Spring*] aye Spring.

It's coming into Spring.

That all looks nicer doesn't it.

And they're going to end up making this place look like a tip. [He means a rubbish tip and he is referring to the other end of the tray.

They say this on the news.

And they're saying Maggie Thatcher should get moving and get all the places done up and that.

And they've removed the pool over to the other side [to the right side] and they've made it a wee land.'

After lunch on the same day, David is uncertain what to put into the tray. After Episode One, water from the pool had been poured into the sand. At the beginning of Episode Three water from inside the boat has been added to it. The sand is very muddy by this time and most of it is covering the entire right-half of the tray. Except for some sand banked around the edges of the left side, it has been completely cleared to reveal the base of the tray. He tried to mop up some of the water by spreading pink paper towels over this area. After several minutes he said:

'I know, I'll put in horses. Guess what I'm doing Miss.'

I am with another child at this time. David is making a star-shaped enclosure with white plastic fences. There aren't enough of them in our room and he goes looking for more from another class. He returns with fences and a big black ape on 'all fours'. He places this in the sand at the right side of the tray. It is looking towards the enclosure. Later that enclosure will contain three small horses. David then finds another small gorilla and adds that to the scene.

Most of the other objects which he used in the first two episodes have been rearranged in the right half of the tray.

'Do you like Sidney Devine [a singer]. My Dad does. I know this one that goes.' *He makes 'da-di-da' sounds then sings the words, 'They took my mother away.'*

David finds another gorilla and is delighted.

'Miss look again. [*Now he has located a small monkey*] Look this wee monkey's got a pal, look they're –'

David places them side by side.

'In that song the boy's name is Jim, he's only five.'

I ask him if he likes horses. [Why, I have no idea.]

'No.' His expression shows distaste.

'They got horses in and that.'

During the course of making these comments, David asked how many episodes he could do and how much film did I have in my camera. Before lunch he informed me Episode Four would be a big fight. After lunch his interest in Episode Three began to fade and he said he didn't think he would do Episode Four.

He wanted an eagle to fly over the scene he had made, and tied wool onto one of the small brown plastic eagles. He held this over one of the houses while I took the photograph.

The following day.

'Episode Four.

Look Miss.'

Two gorillas including a new brown one[26] are together in one corner of the tray.

'All the hospital stuff's been knocked.'

Another boy in the room, remarking on David's tray, tells him it's very nice and very realistic.

'The boat, they managed to get it out and they managed to get it onto the sea and this other wee boat came and helped them.

And then they had a race.

Then the green boat, its engine broke down, it was stuck in the middle of the sea.

Then the police came and said to the driver he shouldn't drive because he couldn't drive a boat and all the people came out to see it.

And then at the end started to clap.

---

[26] On a recent visit to town with me, to choose a toy which he could keep in the room for his own use, he had decided on a brown gorilla in a crouched position. He was delighted because it had been the only one of its kind.

And then went in to celebrate and that's it.
And they had a party all night.
And that's Episode Four.'

KING KONG GETS BURIED

The next story was told by the boy who had been attacked by a big
bird as he tried to get eggs from its nest. He was also the boy with a
strong aesthetic sense and the only one who was markedly disappointed when I stopped taking photographs of the trays. He had
thoroughly enjoyed appraising what he made in photographic form.

An incident which happened outside the unit reflects interestingly on his perception of trays. It happened one very bright sunny
day when he and I were on a trip into town with several other
children. We were walking between rather tall buildings in a
commercial section of the city when he stopped and stared down a
side street. There was a large, newly painted stone building at the
end of it. It had a spire in which there was a gold numbered clock
with a dark blue face and it looked rather unreal against the darker
sandstone of the surrounding structures. He stood for a moment
then exclaimed to us all: 'Look, it's like a tray and we're in it.'

King Kong was one of the most popular of all the creatures and
this was particularly so with the big boys. Although he performed
some amazing feats and met with some astonishing fates, in this
story he quite simply gets buried.

The notes say that the boy who orchestrated King Kong's demise
on this occasion had called into the room the previous day to check
if there would be a tractor available to execute the deed during his
prospective visit. His reasons for waiting a day are not recorded.

On the day the tray was made he ran in to the room and said it
was going to be brilliant and he wanted some milk in either a cup
or a bobo.

'King Kong's deed and they're going to bury him.
All the tractors are going to bury him.
The tractors get two million pounds for burying him. These tractors are
the bestest tractor makers in the whole world.
They are old tractors but they can still move because they're the best.
Everybody liked King Kong 'cos he helped them all the time but he died
'cos he was too high so a aeroplane hit him by accident.

Everybody is at his grave.

They never forget him 'cos he helped them very much so they helped him.

And all the tractors are doing their best to get all the dirt onto him.

And that's the end and he gets buried. Then he gets buried.'

[*I ask if that's it finished.*]

'Wait I'm going to put up a wee cross.

All the tractors are in a line to help them but all the people are round him too and he's not got a cross 'cept a red stick and there are four trees next to him. And these trees were unimportant to him cos he was buried there but nobody'll ever forget him.

That's the end.

I think that tray's best. All his monster friends are there and his two sons too.

Look Miss that's all the monster's friends.

And all they are putting the flowers on it and orange, yellow and white, and that's all.'

THE BRAND NEW BRIDGE

As commented on at the beginning of this section, death was a more prevalent issue than I had appreciated at the time the work took place. It was certainly central to this boy's concerns.

The attractions of fighting and of stealing food, soft drinks, money and toys were already dominant in his life before he came to the unit and began using the room. There was a point with him, as there was with so many of the children, when the attraction of moving off a previously powerful path of conduct comes close to being dropped in favour of taking a different route. At such times the balance between the two can, as the consequence of an awkward intervention or a momentary blunder by an adult, tip the child back onto the old path. In my opinion a moment like this came for him and was lost.

There was no pattern to his use of the room and during his first six months in the unit he would sometimes visit every day for a week, then not at all for a week. The longest interval between visits was about three weeks and when he was in the room he usually stayed for about an hour and made several trays. His favourite, The New Tray, was the closest to the door. On his very first visit he had used it immediately on entering the room. This may well have been a factor in his future preferences.

The first occasion on which he spoke to me about anything personal was at Talk and Draw. It was a rather sudden opening-up in which he told me his granny had died of asthma, that he also had asthma and that he was very frightened of dying. He talked about getting medicine for it and that it would go away when he was older. There was also mention of other family problems, of his father getting angry and his grandfather coming to the house for money which he never gave back. I had been unaware that his grandmother had died, nor did I appreciate until much later the extent to which his whole family had been affected by the loss.

He also said on that occasion: 'Sometimes when I'm out myself I'm scared somebody's going to murder me.'

He said he was upset and that's why he wanted to stay up in the room. Then: 'Nothing else, that's it all oot [out].'

On that day he also made a big tray. This is what he said about it:

'An interesting tray with all the people in the world.

All the vans went away from the caravan site 'cos all the giants come in to sunbathe.'

He didn't return for another seventeen days. When he did, he sat in the cabin with a packet of crisps and a bobo before making a big tray. The main feature was a group of figures standing around a grave. On the grave was a stick and on the stick an army helmet.

'They're all just praying at their friends grave. And all the wee ones are drunk.

The barrow that was used for his grenades is cemented into the ground. The footprints that were around him have cemented up.'

[He used his bobo to make the prints.]

During the following three months, which included the six weeks of the summer holidays when he was not attending the unit, he made eleven visits and produced fourteen trays. They included constructions in which people died and were buried alive, animals attacked each other, clothes went for a swim, motors proceeded sedately along clear roads, soldiers fought cars and, influenced by a movie or video he had seen, a little baby and a big girl got killed.

This next tray story was preceded by a discussion during which I said I had been thinking about him and what he had said to me about his granny and his fear of dying. We considered the possibil-

ity of sharing this with his teacher. He agreed we should do this.
(There is nothing in the notes to suggest why I had chosen to talk
to him directly on that particular day.)

After we had talked he made another big tray and told this story.

'They're walking across the brand new bridge. It just got made there the
now. You can see all the little footsteps, everybody's dancing because they
can do break dancing on the little roof.'

[*He came back up to the room after lunch and continued with the same tray.*]

'There's a pick-up-a-penguin running. There's two ostriches running
across the road chasing two horses.

The deep sea divers drooned [*in a glass sweetie jar*].

His face is bumping up dead high. They've just discovered that he's still
alive.

I've still to put motors on the road and trucks.

The fire brigades zooming across the road.

Oh, a police car's ready to run down two ostriches and they're in luck,
they're across the road now.

That's all.'

[*There was a pause before he continued.*]

'For fuck sake then some cunt's coming. It's only a silly cunt with an
arrow.

The deep sea diver's away back under and there's a traffic jam.

The cars are going beep, beep, beep, beep, beep, beep.

Now I've got to get the gates up.

That's the only place the horse can run.

The gates are going up.

And there's more gates flying up and soon as the horses start running.

The wee baby ponies are in their cage.

There, there.'

[*His teacher has called in to see him.*][27]

'There's other things for tomorrow.

Bridges.

A big giant deer.'

He then moved on to another tray for which there is no photograph.
There were some words:

---

[27] It was not usual for this to happen, unless a child had produced a tray they
considered to be particularly special or if I felt the benefits would outweigh any incon-
venience. It was a need I would have been unable to uphold for everyone who came
to the room and it was mostly an impractical option for the teachers.

'Everybody's died.'
And at the New Tray:
'They're just all fighted and that's all.'
He used several of his favourite figures in a fight which ended with them strewn around the sand, face down, mostly in one corner. From there he stretched out on the mat to play with some cars.
'They're all crashed.'
Back to the big tray.
'People shot all the animals.'
Then, taking off his shoes he climbed into the wooden box on wheels which was kept under one of the big tables.

There is no mention of him having a bobo in there but it would have been highly unlikely if he had not. He had a bobo every day and kept it with him throughout most of his visits, no matter what his activity.

ESCAPE FROM A WATER BOX (2)

The boy who told the next stories has already been introduced. He made extensive use of all the materials in the room, producing trays, paintings, clay models and cardboard constructions. His tray constructions were usually of a quite complex nature involving several areas of special interest. He frequently employed trays and containers within trays. The big tray was again the favourite but he adapted well to whichever one was available. One object which appears more often than any other was a large open shed with a red roof. There was also a wide variation in the consistency of the sand and the extent to which it was shaped and moulded to his needs.
I am presenting four of his stories. Included is the one which involves the escape from the water box and which preceded our Talk and Draw session about his bed-wetting.

'It's going to be all the grass.
The story.
It's a dead dead dead dead busy motorway and up the big big steep hill there are hundreds of houses and in the garage there are big giant trunks and all the fire engines are in there.
And there's water and all that there – and there's grass up the big big hill. And there's a wee swan in the pond and there's a big traffic jam at the left-hand side and at the right-hand side. And nae motor could get under it –

the bridge – because its dead wee and that starts a big big traffic jam and there's a racing motor there and it's trying to get through but it won't get through. And up the tap [top] of the hill there's a farmer's house up there but it's a cottage and the farmer's not got anything he just lives there . He hasn't got any animals.'

I have recorded at this point in the notes that he broke off from tray making and did five paintings. While painting he said he'd got an idea for a tray – an old folks' home.

'Miss. That's a private room.

Have you got any roses?

Up the big hill the people are standing watching all the motors.

And there's a guy with an umbrella and it isn't even rainy.

And there's a lot of shops and houses there.

And doon the bottom of the hill there's a motorway – it's called M8.

It's dead busy because people in the right-hand side want to go across to see the old folks' home to see their granny.

And the people in the left-hand side want to get some food for the old folks home.

And across the motorway there's an old folks' home.

And there's a pond in the garden of the old folks' home and the old granda's sitting in it.

And there's an old granny sunbathing and there are lots of trees and bushes coming out of the house.

And there's somebody just lying there thinking about somebody but I don't know who it is.

And there's a garage in the old folks' home and there's a doctor and a man going to see his Mum.

The two people are shouting at the other old man in the living room because he's hoovering up.

And one man's playing the piano and in the bedroom there's somebody sleeping – just sitting [*long intense pause*] and the other man in the bed is just sitting – a funny way.

And then we go into the last part and that's the bathroom and a man's having a bath and the woman's daeing the toilet – and that's all. I'm finished.'

A polystyrene box in which new wild animals had recently arrived in the room was incorporated into this tray as the old folks' home. I am assuming that the private room he refers to in the story is one of the compartments in the box. Next to the home was a fenced area of imitation grass. There were roads and cars in the centre third of the tray and a bank of sand (the big big hill) covered the right hand third and on this were placed houses, flats, children, various figures and fences.

The third story also relates to events in a big tray.

'Animals are invading the world. It's a prison camp. I had the idea in my bed last night. I'm going to make a big army assault course.

A man does the course then falls out of the tray and dies.

And then the boss came and said 'Come on I'm an expert, I'll dae it with you. The man died but I'm no dying.' He dives in, thinks he's smart, jumps out, jumps over the fence. He thinks he's a pure pervert and takes the ladder with him and dies.

Another does it but he's O.K.'

As this tray was being made, another boy in the room had begun to talk to me about 'pissing the bed'. Usually when a child introduced such an issue I took the opportunity to converse about it in as open a way as possible, and in a voice loud enough to be heard by anyone else in the room who might have a similar difficulty. This was meant to assure them of a sympathetic response if they should ever need to do the same.

After the discussion I decided to take the boy who had introduced the subject back to his class. When I returned, a second big tray was being made. A figure had been placed in a transparent, plastic, water-filled box with a lid. A circle of small play mobile figures were arranged around it. He asked me to write some words for him on a piece of paper.

This was cut to a point at one side before being placed on the sand and directed towards the box. On the paper were the words, 'It is a man escaping from a water box in a big bag.'

The water box was placed in the centre of the left half of the tray. Covering most of the right half was a rectangle formed by fourteen ceramic tiles. On this were two plastic helicopters. Two plastic planes were upside-down in the sand alongside the tiled area.

The story for the tray was this:

'There's an airport right next to it and two aeroplanes flew up in the air doing tricks, turning upside down kidding on they're going to smash into each other.

I think he's smart so the two of them go smash and the two of them are deid [dead].'

GETTING RUN OVER AT THE BUS STOP

This is another story in which an issue was addressed in both a tray and at Talk and Draw during the same visit. It was also a memorable experience for me, mainly for the rather odd way in which monsters were incorporated into it. I never saw anything quite like it again.

A boy I knew quite well, as he had been in my group on my return from the course, came into the room to make a tray about an accident in which he had been involved. He had been knocked down by a bus. In the account he gave, he spoke of a bus, a fence he had held onto and a boy who had run away. That same boy, after being reported to the police, had 'dished in' on one of the windows of his house.

In the centre of the big tray he used two parallel lengths of yellow wooden fences, about eighteen inches long and five inches apart, to depict the road on which the accident took place. These were also placed parallel to the long sides of the tray. Two vehicles – a bus and a truck – were positioned on the road. A male figure lay in front of the truck and another smaller figure was standing at the end of one of the pieces of fence.

I recall watching what happened next with silent astonishment. Whilst my experience with the trays at the time was still very limited, and I was continually being surprised by some of the things the children said and did, I found this a particularly memorable event. After completing the scene, and with no further comment or obvious expression, he quite calmly began to place monsters all over it. A gorilla on all fours was stood on the truck and a large black bat spread over the bus. Around the road itself he put a black curly snake, two black alligators and a green one, which was upside-down.

In a line at the right end of the tray, as if looking on, was a creature which the children referred to as the 'Wompa', the Tyrannosaurus, and the large crab with a black spider on it. A long green snake lay over one section of the fences. Its head and the top eighth of its body were on the road. The rest of it was stretched out in a straight line along the sand. At the front edge of the tray in the centre, the flying horse was balanced on a piece of green painted wooden hedge. This was sticking up vertically in the sand.

This is the story he told.

'It was just at the end bus stop and I got off the bus and said cheerio to the driver and this boy ran after me and I jumped over the fence and ran over. And the bus beeped its horn and that's a' and the truck just hit me and I was holding on the fence, that's a'.'

With the exception of the monsters, the drawing he did was very similar to the scene he had produced in the tray. It had two parallel lengths of fence with two vehicles between them. There was a figure in front of one these and another at one end of a fence. Using his own name to begin the sentence, the words he gave for the picture were: '— got ran over at the bus stop.'

SOOKING AND SOOKING LIKE A MAD MAN

As explained in the example of Talk and Draw entitled 'Tom of the Bumblebees', the main reason Tom's stories have been included is to cover the time when a real feeding-bottle replaced the imitation one. They also illustrate the struggle he was having with his feelings about there being a new baby in the family.

I have chosen to lead in with a piece taken from the notes which I recorded on the day the baby was due to be brought home from the hospital.

Tom poured the water from the grey tray into the big tray. I cleared it up because others might need to use it, but it may have been a wiser option to let him proceed.

He arrived in the room, grabbed a gun and expressed his desire to blast people. I encouraged him to talk and eventually he said his Mum was coming home from the hospital with the baby. We eventually got settled down together and he told me he was worried about what his brothers might do to it.

When I asked if perhaps he was also worried about his own feelings for the baby, he assured me he felt fine. Then, after a pause, he added that he thought the dog would be jealous.

The next visit I want to present took place eight days later.

It began with Tom arriving in the room calling me a 'cow' and calling himself a 'bad boy'. He walked over the tables singing and making noises. I encouraged him down. He sang frantically, continuing to call me a 'cow' and demanding that I leave his tray alone as he began to put stones in The Blue Tray at the Window. He progressed from calling me a 'cow' to repeating the phrase 'anything but a cow', several times.

This was followed by a rendering of a song called 'Don't Sit Under the Apple Tree with Anyone Else but Me'. It's an old song which I like and I asked where he had heard it. Continuing to swear at me he replied 'In a film.' He repeated the song this time changing the end to: 'with anyone else but fucking me'. As he did so, he was shouting and rattling the stones. 'I'm putting all they rocks in.'

He had intended to make an animal tray but changed his mind. He continued singing, with swear-words included, then decided he would like to go out to the garden to get some more stones. On his return he located the small imitation feeding bottle.

'Can I take this downstairs?'
I say it has to stay in the room.
'It gives me a taste of milk.'[28]

He bangs the table and an older girl in the room, with whom he has a friendly relationship, says: 'Is that what you do with your wee brother?' He replied:

'I kick his ba's [balls] in. (BANG BANG.)
All the animals are having a meeting.'
He shoots me in the head.
'I'll blow your brains out.'

He sat with the bottle after 'shooting' his tray and before making some clay flowers. He then tries to copy a miniature cardboard billiard table which the older girl is making. He follows this with another big tray. Two of his favourite characters are at the centre of it.

'Tyrannosaurus and crab.
He's eating him – he's fucking eating him. I'm gonnae kill the bastard. I'm away down, noo.'

During this visit Tom also made a big tray in which all the stones and pebbles were spread over the entire area of sand. In the photograph there is too much sunlight to be able to identify accurately each individual animal, but there seems to be approximately ten of them. Included are lions, an armadillo and a tortoise. These have been placed singly on selected stones. The exception is a small eagle and a horse which are together on one of the largest of them. This is situated near the centre.

Tom made trays very similar to this, but with fewer stones, over a period of about a month when the feelings provoked by the birth of his baby brother were most acute. The majority of the animals he used were wild.

They left a very clear impression which stayed with me for a long time. I sensed that there might be a connection between them and a passage on dispersal which I recalled reading. I eventually relocated it in Melanie Klein's paper 'Envy and Gratitude'. She writes there:

---

[28] There was no aperture in the bottle, nor was there any milk in it.

For instance, I found that concurrently with the greedy and devouring internalization of the object – first of all the breast – the ego in varying degrees fragments itself and its objects, and in this way achieves a dispersal of the destructive impulses and of internal persecutory anxieties. (Klein, [1957] 1984, p. 191)

It was between that visit and the next, two days later, that I acquired a real feeding-bottle. At this early stage in its use, the routine of bringing in milk had not been established and on this occasion it would have been filled with water.

As the visit began a boy from another class, passing by the room, looked in to show he had a CB radio. Tom was distracted by this and wanted to try it. I suggested the passer-by go back to his class and Tom was not pleased with me. 'My dog's very angry with you. I could have got a girlfriend on the CB.' He then proceeds to work on his tray and to tell a story for it.

'All the animals are friends.'
He places a few lions in the sand. [I have noted that I foolishly mention something about needing more trees for the room.] Tom says I have given him a brilliant idea and begins to make another tray.
'I'm full of screams.'
He reminds me of a café we had visited a long time ago. He had been invited to join my group on one of our frequent visits there. He is singing frantically, littering the song with swear-words.
'I'm gonnae boot your ba's [balls].
I'm gonnae kick you fucking arse.'
I ask who it is he's feeling so angry with. It is his brother Gordon.
'Greedy wee fucking bastard.'
Tom places trees and cones very carefully all over the tray and puts in the big crab and the big Tyrannosaurus.
'These two are fighting – and knocking every single one of these trees down.'
Tom then wanted to make something out of boxes. We talk a bit about the baby. Tom says it pukes up all over his Ma. He asks if he can fill the baby's bottle and drinks out of it. He sucks the feeding bottle and tells me his Ma said to the baby, 'You're a greedy, greedy boy.' The bottle is refilled and drunk continually. When he finishes the bottle he says:
'I'm a greedy, greedy boy.'
He wants more but I suggest it is about time for him to go back down to class. He suggests he makes another tray and has another drink. I go along with this – reluctantly. He has been with me for an hour and ten minutes. He makes a carpet tray – with a baby in it.
'You're a greedy greedy boy – the mummy will come in and say. Rock a bye baby on the tray.'

He has placed the baby in a pale blue plastic rocker.
'Miss, there's my tray.'
The baby is sitting in the rocker getting fed by Tom.
'He's sooking and sooking like a mad man, sooking and sooking.'
He begins to squeeze water on the baby's face then decides to wash it by giving it a shower with the water from the bottle.
'Now the doctor's coming to take the baby. Ay wee baby shit all over the doctor.'

I note that I had great difficulty getting Tom to return to his class that day!

SAUSAGE, EGG AND BEANS, FOUR TIMES

The following stories were told by the boy who did the drawing 'Sending a Message Up to Space'. They have been wrapped up with another of the visits which contributed to his feeling more at ease with me. I have sufficient supplementary notes to be able to illustrate something of our interaction on that occasion. I became increasingly less tentative about making the kind of intervention described here, as my confidence in the work grew. From those notes it is also apparent that my decision to declare my concern and encourage him to spend more time in the room had been arrived at through discussion with his class teacher.

The visit in question began with a tray which had the following story.

'The Indians and Cowboys are fighting because the cowboys want the Indian's land.
    That's it.
    They're meant to be apaches.'

He then sat at the big desk[29] to play with some plastic figures which he particularly liked. These had movable joints at the neck, shoulders and the hips, and he usually put them through a series of routines which combined a mixture of fighting and acrobatics. On the day

---

[29] Children were not usually allowed to sit at the big desk, but there were occasional exceptions providing the occupant was amenable to moving elsewhere immediately, if it was required for Talk and Draw.

in question he slapped them around with such vehemence that I was startled several times by the sound of them impacting against each other.

After this he moved on to the cabin and it was while he was sitting in there and I was crouched outside that I spoke to him.

I said I had been thinking about him a lot and that I thought deep inside there were things which worried him and were making him sad. He said 'Rubbish, I don't know what you're talking about' and began to turn the car-wheel in the cabin quite frantically. This activity lasted for several minutes. In some trepidation I remained where I was, and when he had quietened down slightly, I continued in a similar vein. He responded by saying, 'I don't know what you're talking about.'

I then suggested that he might come up to see me every day and that perhaps I could help him. In the notes I have added, 'help with what I didn't say'. I was then needed elsewhere in the room. He began singing a little, made two trays, stayed around, came back in the afternoon, was very vociferous and said he'd hundreds of things to 'get out'. He then proceeded to have a thoroughly good swear.

Four days later, over a two-day period, he made several trays which featured some of his more violent themes. Here are two of them:

'God has made it rain stones and shells and the guys are still fighting – it's fucking nane [none] of them have been killed.
So they're still fighting like fuck.
And that's it.'

And using the blue tray at the window:

'I'm putting it [the 'Minotaur'] in his mouth [the Tyrannosaurus] as tho' he's bleeding.
The two snakes are fighting for the eagle and that big monster's eating that guy and he's bust all his tummy open.
And his pal's on his back and there's hundreds of skeletons about because of those guys and [*he used two words which I did not hear*] puking a horse up and flies – just waiting for the scraps – and he's the big guy's wee boy and he's gonna get the one that falls and that's it.'

It was eight months after this that he talked to me about his father who had left the family home when he was a baby. He also spoke of the feelings which he, and the other members of his family, had about this and other major events in their lives. The same day at

Talk and Draw he did the first of what became a series of pictures. It is from these that I took the title 'Sausage, Egg and Beans, Four Times'. They were produced over a nine-day period and were initiated entirely by him. Technically they belong with the examples of Talk and Draw but placed here they help to illustrate the relationship between the two procedures.

Apart from a few family scenes in the carpet tray, the domestic relationships portrayed in these four pictures were very unlike all the wild and warring dramas which he had usually produced. Knowing how painfully defended he was, they they have a special charm for me.

In the first story the Da walks in the door, sits down, watches the telly, turns it off, goes to bed and wakes up with the sun shining in when he opens the curtains. Then the Ma walks in, turns on the cooker and makes sausage, egg and beans. Then the wee boy wakes up and goes to school. The words with which he concluded were:

> 'I'll need to draw the wee boy noo [now] as if he's going out of the door. There that's it.'

In the next one, which he did the following day, he said:

> 'The Da walks in. The Ma's in the bed. The Da walks over to the cooker which I've still to draw. He puts the cooker on and makes sausage, beans and egg. Yesterday the Ma done it for the Da but today the Da's doing it for the Ma. And I'm going to have to draw a wee Da here.
> She gets up and puts the radio on.
> That's the radio.
> Then the Ma and Da sit down and have sausage beans and eggs.'
> *I ask if he has ever done drawings like these before and he says no.*
> 'Then they start watching the telly – four knobs because there's four channels.'

Two days later:

> 'The wee boy walks in the hoose and the Ma and the Da are in bed. When you're doing things you've got to do them right especially good things like this. The wee boy turns on the telly and he goes out to the cooker and he makes sausage, beans and eggs.'

Five days on, as he begins to draw a similar picture, I ask if the scene is different from the others.

'Aye. Mummy and Daddy in bed. Little boy comes in. The Mummy and Daddy are in bed, the wee boy goes in makes sausage, beans and eggs. That's it.'

It was another three months after this that he made a big tray and said about it:

'It's my best ever.
They poodles are too big.
It's just a farmyard at eight o'clock in the morning. The farmer's going out to plough the fields in his tractor and his wife is going to milk the cows, to milk and feed the cows actually. And then the gran is going to feed the horses and pigs and sheeps and the little girl is going to feed the dogs.
The little skunk that is running up the side of the field sees something to eat. It is a field mouse.
The farmer is going an important message before he ploughs the field.
He is going to fly his plane to the supermarket which is 130 miles away.
Then the gran will go in the car to the grain farm and the little girl will then use her motor bike to take a letter round to the farm. And the wife is going to train the horses and she is going out to buy a new dog today.
It is a border collie. She thinks she will be good for rounding up the sheep.
The scarecrow is getting old and tattery so the man is going to put some old clothes on it and make it a new face.
And that's it.'

A PROFESSOR WHO WAS MAD ON SPORTS CARS

Here are two stories with a different agenda. They are being included as a means of introducing another of the issues which I think deserves some space. It emerged quite early on in the work but was side-stepped at the time. To have followed it up then, to the extent it deserved, would have taken me away, for too long, from the journey I was already on.

It relates to the reading difficulties of a big boy who had joined my group shortly after I returned to the unit. With no specialist training in remedial reading, my general approach to children who had problems had always been extremely basic. Backed by a large measure of persistence and personal enthusiasm I usually attempted, as thoroughly as possible, to identify an approach which worked for that particular child. With the big boys in particular, and this boy was probably the biggest with whom I worked, this often entailed leading them into a kind of reading regression. During this I would advocate, with as much conviction as I could muster, that going back to the little easy words was the best way of working back up to the big ones. If this did not slowly and surely begin to work for them, I usually sought help and advice from an 'expert'.

The success of such an approach obviously requires a large amount of trust on the part of the child and an absolute insistence by the worker that no one in the group will be allowed to do or say anything which would undermine the child's efforts to address the problem. Taking up such a position is of course extremely reassuring for everyone present, whether they can read or not. This same attitude was adopted in relation to any other concern which a child might risk revealing in the presence of others.

This boy, whose difficulties provoked a lively if short-lived focus on some of the factors which can influence a child's attitude to reading, was receiving special remedial help within the unit. He was supposed to be unable to read.

It was shortly after joining my group that he constructed a tray and told this story about it.

'There was a professor who was mad on sports cars. He made a contraption that stole racing cars and kept them behind lots of fencing and bricks.

He got them in the fencing by making a hole in the ground and driving them through.

The hole would get covered up at night so no one could get their cars back.'

When he told the story I wrote it down roughly in my notebook. This was customary practice with all the children. Then, responding to his obvious pleasure in the story, he agreed to my suggestion that I make a copy of it for him. This was not something I usually did with the tray stories, but I considered this a special occasion and reproduced it in my best printing. When I handed it to him later, he took the story from me and read it fluently.

Later the same day he made another tray and wrote a sequel. I also wrote that one out and he read it just as easily.

'The professor made a car out of all the other cars.

The car could go back in time so he tries the car out and it works. So now he lives back in time.'

The possibility that the tray stories might be useful to other children with reading difficulties made it difficult for me to let the matter drop completely. I made several attempts to deposit it in the lap of others with an interest in the subject. And I did co-operate for several weeks with another teacher in the unit who had two boys in her group diagnosed as having severe reading difficulties. We compiled books for them, using photographs of their trays as illustrations at the top of the pages and with the stories written out underneath.

The children's ease with their own stories was in marked contrast to the difficulties which they continued to experience when faced with a printed book – even when the words presented there were simpler than their own. There are no doubt numerous informed reasons why this should be so but based on my own observations two issues were of interest.

I assumed that the tray stories, relating as they often did to issues which had a powerful if unrecognised significance for the child, provided a boost which helped carry them over some of the conscious blocks they had acquired in the process of learning to read with a big 'R'. Also I recalled working with several children who, when faced with a new book, exhibited a resistance which suggested not only the weariness of the failed reader, but a real fear of what might be encountered in the text. Reading one's own story circumvents this particular problem. Not reading at all would obviously be an even more effective defence against coming across an unpleasurable trigger.

I found a book called *The Treatment of the Child in Emotional Conflict* by Hyman S. Lippman[30] which offers some support for this second proposition.

> In their work with children, Sylvester and Kunst (1943:69) found a specific connection between reading disability and the evolution of the exploratory function. These children lacked the courage for the active curiosity which is required to master reading. Sylvester and Kunst found that, when the child's zeal to explore was blocked, he often interpreted exploration as unacceptable and dangerous. If, on the other hand when the exploratory function was overindulged, the child also found exploration threatening, presumably because he had seen more than he could assimilate without anxiety. Reading then became a danger that had to be avoided. (Lippman, 1956, p. 187)

---

[30] This book had been influenced by principles of therapy as developed at the Amherst H. Wilder Child Guidance Clinic in St Paul, Minnesota. Hyman Lippman, who had worked there, had also received a psychoanalytic training in Vienna, in which seminars with Anna Freud had played a part.

As with the emotional difficulties of the big boys, so with the reading ones; better that they should be dealt with at a time when both the child and the problem are still quite small.

TRYING TO GET UP TO NEW YORK

These tray stories and comments from 'Master Eeps' can give only a glimpse of the idiosyncratic nature of his ideas and concerns. Although animals and dinosaurs made appearances in his early trays, and he had brief encounters with them throughout his use of the room, the materials around which his inventiveness mainly revolved were flat plastic blocks. The majority of these were yellow and orange, some smaller ones were purple; others with sloping sides were red and excellent for making roofs. They could be fitted together to construct flats and houses; when not being used as buildings they were usually employed as tiles which he set out like coloured patios in the sand. One of the most interesting buildings he constructed was a block of flats with a central tower and a plasticine angel on top. Two separate stems of foliage, in stands, were set at each corner of it and the finishing touch was a shaft of light from the sun which he reflected onto them using a tin lid.

Many of the features which he produced in and around his trays were a delight to him. He was one of the first children to enjoy using cotton wool, and on one occasion enhanced some of the flats he had made by placing a 'cloud' of it on top of them. To this he added a small black Playmobile figure. It was a striking construction, begun only four minutes before it was time for him to go home. There was no story for it.

Another tray in which he used cotton wool as a cloud is the subject of the next story. In it, a small figure on a motorcycle is traversing the sand from right to left. There are skyscrapers at the back of the tray and just behind and to the left of the rider, a light brown panther is lurking in a bundle of cotton wool.[31]

'Look at the size of New York.
New York skyscrapers.
A panther climbing up on the clouds – the wee guy was trying to get up to New York.'

---

[31] This feature is included in the selection of colour photographs between pages 116 and 117.

The frequency with which the plastic blocks appear in these examples of his stories here is commensurate with the frequency of their appearance in the whole of his tray work.

'It's a nice wee tray isn't it.
That's their houses [*he is referring to two small boy figures*].
The wind blew the flats about and you could see them moving a bit.
And the storm rose across them and knocked them down. And all the people got damaged and everybody's brains were dead and everybody's brains were covered with sick.
The wee boys rescued them from sinking and that was the end of the big high rising.
And something else happened in there.
Everything went all back to normal at last because the two boys rescued and stood them back up and saved the mother, all the policeman and the mother.
And then the world came back to water again, [*?water*] normal and watery.'

The story was told as he poured water over the high rise flats. He had moved these, during the course of the story telling, from the big tray into a small water tray.

About a month later he made a line of roads running from right to left, dissecting the whole area of the big tray. The plastic blocks were there as flats and houses.

'I'm putting the big bad fences round the factory so that boys can't break in. Because if they break in the alarm will just go off. That's the adventure playground.'
There is a small group of small dinosaurs above the road in the top right quarter of the tray.
'This is a boy [*a blue plastic man*].
It's a clever tray isn't it.
The Ninjas are sad because you have to take the tray down. [*It is not recorded in the notes why or if this was so.*]
One of them is lying down.
The two of them have got their heads down because you're taking ...
That'll make them very sad and they'll jump about and they've got special power to turn the dinosaurs into real monsters.
He'll put his laser beam on it and all the dinosaurs are real now. Then the big Daddy one comes.
Then I've took it down. It's too late to build it back up.

That's just like the story of war.'
He dismantles the tray and puts everything away to prevent me taking a photograph. Again the notes do not explain why this was so.

I am including the next story because it is short and sweet, and probably seemed so at the time.

'I left my sweary words outside in the bin on Thursday.
Miss, I'm going to make a fresh start.
I'm making a big pyramid for the flats to stand on.'

Six weeks, nineteen visits and twenty-three trays later: this time he worked in The Dry Tray at the Window. He had built flats and two short lines of houses with a space between them. In the story he referred to the space as a lane. The marbles he mentioned are made of steel. There were four of them.

'These marbles are destroyers.
Look at the wee lane.
If you want to go to the flats you have to go through the wee lane bit.
Look at that deseen. [design].
I love you.
Look they destroyers are up there.
They're burying in the sand, you have to get them up there.
The destroyers are moving in on us.
The big one's the leader.
Look what the destroyer's done. The destroyers took the flats to pieces.
They had a plan – the people in the flats made a plan to destroy the destroyer.
So he made a trap in the ground, so one of them jumped and got caught and one of them jumped in and got caught and another one – all them jumped in and got caught.
Then the stupid destroyers put sand all over the building but they couldn't reach the high block of flats.
Look at all the sand. It's all over the roofs.
I've got hundreds of parts, the parts are up to a hundred.
Doesn't that place look different. [*The houses have been covered with sand.*]
I'd better go and get Godzilla, see if they can tackle him. [*Godzilla is his name for the big Tyrannosaurus Rex.*]
He's Pegasus [*he is referring to the flying horse*] – his name isn't Pegasus anymore, he's Tyrannosaurus's friend.

The Tyrannosaurus starts to come in. Look, fuck, that's huge. [*He compares the size of Tyrannosaurus to the size of the flats.*]

He's turning his nose into it. And he looks down and he sees destroyers hitting him and Tyrannosaurus destroys one of the destroyers. And he tries to hit Pegasus and he kills it and Tyrannosaurus gets angry and Tyrannosaurus lifts Pegasus up on his head the – he's a she – she's up and Tyrannosaurus – they're playing with each other.

Next minute the destroyers started to come out. The Tyrannosaurus moved his head and came through that bit and shut his mouth and jaw and killed it.

Then he puts his tail through the floor under the concrete as well and moves the flats.

Then the destroyers threw the sand all over Tyrannosaurus and Pegasus got his paws and crushed it to fuck.

And the big one is angry and wallops Tyrannosaurus on the head and Tyrannosaurus knocks down the flats and he's knocked them all down.'

The next tray was his first after the summer holidays. It was a very dry one. The flats featured again. He began the tray with them.

'There's a thunder storm and there's a wee bomb trying to wrap round the chimney.

[?] The flats are cold. There's a thunder and there's snow and the slates are getting too slidey. [*He has drawn them on the roof with chalk.*]

The Concorde landed and the other jet's landed and the other one.

That's all.'

Several days before the next tray story he began using some of the dogs we had recently acquired. Children were usually seduced away from using their favourite objects when new ones were introduced to the room. Unless a very strong attachment was formed, the return to the objects of their previous affection was usually quite speedy. Not long after the dogs had ceased to be a novelty the new pack of wild animals had arrived and Master Eeps transferred to using these in two trays, before reverting back to his usual materials.

The next tray was his first substantial one involving animals. He also made use of water containers, which were not a regular feature of his constructions.

'There's the seals swimming with the penguins.

That's all.

They two wee tigers see the wee baby male elephant.

The big elephant killed the wee baby male.

The other one's dead and the seals trying to help them by burying them.

And they went and buried one of the wee tigers. It was just a baby.

And the seal's guts were hanging out, the guts ripped out.

The two other seals had their guts ripped out and this seal said the messy mother of shite.

And the rest of the animals were upset about the seal.

And see how the penguins they died.

And the wee seal's upset. Look at his head bowing, he's crying – look at his tears [*water dripping off*].

All the other animals over there were crying.

Even the giraffe came over and had a look. He put his head down.

And they buried the wee penguins in the other big water and put the other seals in the water.

Look at him [*the seal*] upset. He's very upset swimming backwards.

I wonder why he's upset. [*He wants me to say. I pass it back to him.*]

He was upset because his pals were away.

And [*he mentions my name*] comes along and sees the wee dolphin crying in the water.

And [*he mentions me again*] comes over to the water and she says something. [*I again pass it back to him.*]

Oh I'm sorry poor sorry seal.

And you say come with me and I'll look after you.

And you put him in this tray and when you came you saw he wasn't really dead at all – the penguins weren't really dead and he got a shock.

And when you came in you just put him in the water tray and he was happy there and his pals were there and wee pals were licking him because he was very good and you put him in the water.

He [*the seal*] found something wrong with the water and you came over and you said oh no.

And the – I – the wee seal – got his tail and put the wee penguins in to keep them safe – saved them.

And look at the water, it's rot. It's rotting away and those gremlins came, those fucking gremlins and all the animals ran away to shit.'

This story was brought to a 'false' close as Master Eeps became aware that one of the other children was listening attentively to his story.

A week before his last visit to the room he made what was probably the best designed and ordered of all the trays. In this one he had used the plastic blocks as tiles in the sand. (An optimistic view would be that it reflected a spread of internal order rather than just an attempt to achieve some.)

Using his favourite dry tray, the main feature was a rectangular formation made up of twenty-eight plastic blocks. At the centre of it was a row of adjoining flats, one of which was topped with a turret. This was all enclosed within a complete square of green and yellow wooden fences. Down the left side, pieces of green foliage were stuck upright in the sand, and hard up against the frame of the tray were green wooden hedges. He said:

'Look at that tray. It's marvellous.

The guys did work on the sides of the buildings and the back wall and the front and they've done it all with tiles in the walls and the ceilings and it's got all nice wallpaper.

And you get one hell of a view and you can see the red road flats.[32]

Are you sure about that – write that. And when you put brackets round it that's the angry voice of the deadly guy who hates everybody. He's a worker and he's got something to do with all the killings about here.

And if the arsehole strikes again we'll have to do something about it and the polis [police] station is just down the road.

And the wee guy said on the bike we'll never stop the bastard then we'll kill his fucking dog for all we care.'

All I have recorded for his last visit are these words,

'I'll be saying goodbye to the flatsies soon.'
And a moment later,
'I hate the feeling.'

BEDTIME FOR GOODNESS

The last words belong to Ruth. She is the child who, in 'Three Early Encounters', was identified as having used the phrase 'I'm getting out my worries'. She was also more responsible probably than anyone else for establishing the room as a place where worries could be brought. The irony is that those she did bring were, for far too long, not understood sufficiently for them to be alleviated. There will be more about this in a moment.

If it is accepted that the majority of the boys who attended the unit should have been given help long before their difficulties had reached a chronic stage, then it applies just as much with the girls. I cannot think of any of those with whom I worked who would not

---

[32] This is a name used for a particular group of flats in the city.

have responded extremely well to an opportunity to use the kind of facility being advocated here while attending their own local school.

Three of the four girls who used the room extensively, during the most active phase of its development, had been, or were being, sexually abused and, as indicated in 'Three Early Encounters', she was one of them. She was also the first of the three to get far enough through the more acute distress, which preceded disclosure, to be able to assist the other two in addressing their experiences. The girls had much in common as regards their response to the abuse and, by presenting a virtually complete block of her stories, she will be both representing them and helping to compensate for a bias which has so far been in favour of the boys. They were recorded during the first four months of her visits to the room.

Very few children attended the unit for as long as she did. She was there for just over three-and-a-half years, and when she did move on it was to attend a mainstream primary school in another district. The change was precipitated when she went to live with a new foster family. She was ten-and-a-half when she left.

The abuse from which she suffered was being perpetrated by her father even as he was attending meetings in the unit to arrange for her admission. On these occasions he expressed very plausibly his deep concern about her past insecurities, and declared his dedication to her future stability and welfare. This plausibility was a major contributing factor to the confusion experienced by all the workers involved in the case as we attempted to discover what could be happening at home, and what might be responsible for causing a child such profound distress. Neither before nor since have I known a child to be so upset.

Numerous visits to the child's home by a social worker who had known the father for years, and who was unable to entertain the idea that he could have abused his daughter, added to the confusion. Nothing was forthcoming which might have helped clarify the situation and we were thrust time and again towards the view that, whatever was troubling her, it had no basis in reality. Yet, as will be apparent from the material which follows, she could hardly have given us clearer signals of being in need of help and, as we realised after gaining more experience, of what issues were involved.

She had also had a rootless sort of existence, having been abandoned by her mother at least four times before she reached the age of two. As she had started out, so she had continued. It had certainly left her with some rather odd perceptions of the world and the people in it, and trying to separate out the effects of abuse from manifestations of an extremely disrupted upbringing complicated the situation even further. It was as if the abuse had rocketed through an already shaky system, transforming slightly odd behaviour into the decidedly bizarre.

It is interesting to note that in the seven years preceding the setting up of the environment, sexual abuse had not once been identified as a factor in the behaviour of any of the children who had attended the unit. Yet from this time on, there were occasions when more than 50 per cent of the children were struggling with experiences which had a serious sexual component. The establishment of a facility in which such issues were more likely to emerge coincided with a universally increased awareness of the issue.

Ruth's first visit to the room was made about a month after she came to the unit. There was a two-week interval between each of her first three visits, with the next seventeen being made at intervals varying from one to seven days. The majority of these occurred every day or every other day.

Over the entire duration of her stay in the unit she produced so many trays, paintings, drawings and constructions featuring phalluses of varying characteristics and proportions I came to associate the term 'The Persistent Phallus' with the complete record of her work. As regards the policy of leaving the children to make their own connections between the real and the symbolic, the only overt one she made was between a clay object and a penis, months after disclosing the abuse. As she was about to leave the room one day, she turned back for a moment to appraise a long thick object which she had made, and which was lying on the table near the door. With an air of slight surprise she looked me straight in the eye and remarked, 'You know what that looks like, don't you?' – or words to that effect. She then proceeded immediately on her way.

I was unable to make a reasoned appraisal of what effect this might have had on her, or to monitor changes in what she subsequently produced. The incident coincided with a move to a different class and the development of a relationship which in many respects began to provide much of what she had been finding with me in the room. It was a positive development for her and she began to visit less frequently.

These concluding stories and dreams are undoubtedly some of the most distressing that were told. They are a chastening reminder of the distress which some children experience for far too long while adults, even with the best will in the world, but with insufficient information and experience, fail to provide the help that they need.

The cut-off point for this selection has been chosen so that I can end with the words she gave for a mandala. At least I have assumed it to be one. I made some unexpected connections after deciding to do this, and these will also be commented on as this section is drawn to a close.

On her very first visit, Ruth made a big tray in which the only feature was a bridge with two small wooden ladders leaning against it. There was a red-and-white life-ring on top. The sand had not been altered or moulded in any way.

She made her next tray two weeks later.

In the photograph of the finished construction there is a cage made with green metal fences. It had contained an elephant but during the course of making the tray, the elephant was moved out into a space by itself and its place taken by a gorilla. A cow and a camel are in open enclosures at either side of the cage. This is overlooked by two Mounties. There is also one Mountie at each of the four corners of the tray. In no special formation, as far as I can see, there are some houses, cars, traffic signs, a flag, a tree and a lighthouse.

'It's an elephant's cage and a horse's cage. Two animals, that's better.
He's in a – he's locked in, he can still get out.
Look an elephant and two animals.
What's that? [laughs – it's a camel].
Can I put in some of these?
[She puts in the Mounties.] To stop people sneaking up on the animals.
Someone could sneak up and sneak the animals.
There's that elephant trapped there.
Look Miss whatever your name is. [A fence has been placed on top of the fenced-in elephant.] All the animals are going for a sleep now.
Do you know what that thing's there for?
That car's stuck.
Can I put in some houses.
This is for the animals to go for their tea. [She hammers the metal cage, crash bang.]
[?] The elephants come out because the gorilla's gone in.'

Two weeks later:

'The budgie's [*an ostrich*] in the garden playing with the rocking horse when the sink was water.

They are bricks [*segments of cane*] to stop the ladder from falling down.

The wee dog's watching the man playing the piano.

The bed is walking upstairs.

The baby's in bed sleeping.

The toilet's beside the baby's cot.

The chair's breaking.'

[*At this point she was invited to a previously scheduled swimming class.*]

A further two weeks on she made a cardboard boat with the top of a box and with some smaller boxes inside. She called it a 'robay boat'. Two days later:

'There's the wardrobe.

The men are fighting.

And they're sitting down watching them Mr T. and B.A.

And they two are the babies and that's the bonfire and the table.

That's the kennel and it keeps jumping up and down on the roof.

That's it.'

From then on the visits became more frequent and over the next nine days another three trays were made. There are no stories for these. On the tenth day this was the story:

'The robot's standing watching the army men pointing to the one that he likes and the two orange men were dancing.

And the two men are marching.

The monkey's trying to fall off the tree.'

Five days later:

'Miss, it's a secret. I'll need to whisper in your ear.

It's a hutch for a car park.

Story. [*This could be her word or mine.*]

The roads crashed and the houses have tumbled over.

The motor's trying to get out of there and they're crashing into the door.

And one of them got out.

That's a'.'

And the next day:

'It's a secret.'
? What's happening.
'The sand castle's going to fall down in five minutes.
And they're all going to say watch out because they're all going to jump and say it's all dirty because it's all dirty.'
In the water tray she is using the dolphin to squirt water. She also makes clay sausages.

The following day she made five trays and did a painting. Where this came in the order of things is not recorded. It consisted of five vertical strokes of paint surrounded by scores of daubs of the same colours: red, blue, brown and yellow.

This is the story for the first tray:

'The snakes biting me and it's climbing all over the house where the wee houses are –
And it's lying on top of the witch and it's cuddling the dragon and picking up the spider and trying to bite the crab's body and it's trying to get the alligator.
And that's all.'

The second story:

'The spade has hanged upside down.
The chimney's got the water in it.
And there's a man inside the water to stop him from getting wet.
And the flower's upside down.
And the trees are going to slip because it's a windy day and the school's gonnae fall down.
That's going to fall down – look it's leaning sideways.'
She could be referring here to numerous objects. In the tray there was a red shed, Tyrannosaurus, a big green grasshopper, a witch, a black spider, two small dinosaurs, a house and a black snake lying across the big plastic crab.
'I've got a nicer tray with lots of flowers.'
She wanted to take the boots off an Action Man. They were the only articles of clothing on him.
'Look at them flying.'
This Action Man was joined by another, also naked, and placed on a large, red-plastic vehicle which was usually referred to by the children as the 'He-Man machine'.

The two bare men also make an appearance in the next tray. One is sitting in the sand beside some foliage and the other is at the top of a small vertical piece of cardboard tubing, about ten inches long. Directly behind this is a much longer piece of tube. This is also standing vertical in the sand.

Between her making this tray and moving on to the next, a boy in the room tells me a dream and she says:

'I've got a dream.
I think I'm going to die. And my wee brother[33] thinks he's going to die. And he thinks he's going to die again and again and again. [*Pause*].
I could think that I'm going to sleep at night time and I hope I – and John doesn't crash.
That's all.'

There is no indication whether 'John' is someone she knows, or is a boy of that name in the unit.

This is the third story:

'The horse is dying for help and the houses are in [the shed] to stop him from dying.
And that's all.'

The fourth story was:

'The houses were there because the fire engines were there as well and the ones were all dying because the houses were tap dancing away.'

In the fifth tray there was an elephant and a horse in an enclosure and an upturned pink bath in the middle of the sand.

'They're having a bath and they're in the boat. And the boat's gone to England to pick up other animals.'
Rain outside is blowing against the windows.
'Tear drops are falling on the window.'

Four days later she produced a tray and a painting of two houses. One of the houses is larger than the other and has a black roof, no windows and no doors. The other has a red roof with blacked-in

---

[33] She did not have a wee brother nor was there a child associated with her family whom she might have considered to be one.

windows and no door. There is a path leading up to this one. In her tray the big crab has a black spider spread over the top of it.

'It's a secret story. I'll tell you when nobody's there.

The crab's in the bed. The monkey's watching the houses for the children.

And this [*the Tyrannosaurus*] is trying to sleep but it's not because people are crying.

And he's biting somebody's head.

The two houses are far far far far far far away.

That's all.

[*Pause.*]

And the monkeys and the elephants are happy now.

I forgot to tell you about this. [*She is referring to the spider.*] The wee spider's climbing up my hand.'

The next day she wanted a cover for her tray so that no one could see what she was making.

'This giraffe is going to see all the wee baby cows and then he's going over to eat his dinner.

And the wee silver one [*a reindeer*] is going over to see the elephant, then after that he's going to see the scunner [*a black bull*] and everyone of them are marching.

The elephant's first and then the pigs and the cows and then the monkey.

And I forgot the wee scunner and he's sitting beside the cow.

That's all.'

[*A horse is walked along the floor and she says:*]

'He's deid.'

[*I ask what's going to happen now.*]

'His friend will get him up.

He dies again.'

I have made a note that 'two friends' are also 'walked' and that this routine is repeated several times.

In a third tray there was the 'Minotaur' and the flying horse. She described them as monsters and said they were fighting, then added that there was no story.

The next day two trays were made. As the story was being told for the first of these, she began to clear it away.

'The two men are going on to their seals and they are going to go away to London Zoo to see them and one of them are going away and one of them's lost.

And you can see their footprints.

And the men are pressing the fire buttons.

The fire buttons are going tick tock and the fences are going away and the zebra's up in the tree.

And the flowers are in the zebra's home.

And the two donkeys are far far far away from here now. And that's all. It's all greasy. There that's what I've left.'

A second story was then told around the same tray.

'These two scarecrows [reindeer] are trying to watch the horses the dogs the pigs.

One of them are going into it. The other one's kicking the sand.

He's knocking all the things down and the little donkey his friend they're away home now to go to sleep.

And the pigs are all in beside the donkey and the horses.

They've the gates and they've locked the gates up.

And they're all happy now.

And they've got walls beside them to stop them [the reindeer] from falling and they're friends now.

That's all. Goodnight.

And plus they're getting in a bath.

And both of them are getting in the same bath.

And that's all.'

All that remained in the tray after the story had been told was a mixture of cows and horses lying around in a long wooden pencil-box. Two large reindeer were lying on their sides in the sand and there was a Mountie a few inches away lying face up in the sand.

During the same visit she had also used The Blue Tray at the Window. There is no story for this, but in the photograph taken when she had finished with it one can see a mess of stones, a bridge, yellow wooden fences and green metal ones. Lying over these on their backs are frogs and alligators. In the top left corner are several half-buried skeletons, and in the lower left corner, where the sand has been scraped away, there is a patch of Alcan foil. On this is sitting a white polar bear. Another polar bear is in the sand a few inches away in a space by itself. She often used these white polar bears to represent herself and her sister. That day she also told me a dream.

'Monsters in my room. They were fighting and making noises and I couldn't get to sleep.

And a giraffe was in my room and it was tickling me and feeling me and seeing if I was a monster.

And feeling me – and licking me and pretending that I was a monster – that he was a –

And I was feeling so hot that I woke up. And there was nobody there and I went to sleep and they came back again.

And a big huge monster came – huge like bigger than a house came in and tickled and tickled you and he said to his other pals come on we'll tickle her again.

And he said that he'll take us into his motor and kill him.

I was thinking that they were going to batter me.

And then I woke up and all I saw was a bare room.

And I thought there was something in it – saw a giraffe under my bed – ignored him – trying to batter me and wouldn't and he said who are you and me and [she names her sister] said we didn't want to – you. And somebody was in.'

A visitor came into the room. After the interruption she asked me if I wanted to know her sister's dream, and continued:

'Because [she] was sleeping they all said let's go up to the house and tickle her and laugh and play tickling her and saying that they would like to play with her.'

Several times she spoke about her father, who had said not to let the monsters into her room. She added that they had been in her room but now they were in her sister's.

'I'm going to smack every one of your bottoms. You should get the monsters out. Don't do that again because it –

For your information Mum we're not doing that again and that's OK Mum and why have we got to do what you tell us. She said just be quiet and get to sleep and we said hope –

And my Mum said you'd better move your bum.

And we said why have you got to say that?

And they went like the why. And they kept saying why why why why why.

And kept saying why why and they said just go and get to sleep and if you dae I'll be your friend and they did it.

And my Mummy's dream and my Dad's.

My Mum was dying that's all.

And Dad was dying and that's all goodnight.
That's all.'

The following morning she was waiting for me in the room when I arrived. She said she had another dream to tell me.

'I went in the sitting room and I seen my Dad's fag burning and then when I went to tell him the house was on fire.
And that's all.'

Later she told me she was feeling excited because it was Easter and she would be getting an egg. After this she made a big tray and wanted to invite her teacher to see it. She told the story of it to him. He recounted it to me later. There was only one feature in the tray. It was a cardboard tube about two feet long standing vertically in the centre of the sand. Two pieces of wood and four ridges of sand fanned out from its base and in two of the spaces between them sat a large frog.

'There was a chimney and Jesus is being crucified and there's nothing in the chimney and you can look in the chimney and see that there's nothing in it.'

Then it was the Easter holidays and eleven days had passed before she made her next visit. In the deep tray an animal had been caged using the green metal fences. There is no reference in the story to the animal and in the photograph its identity is disguised by the fences. She said:

'There's no story for it. I'll tell you about the fences. They're upside-down.
And the invisible animals are moaning and the doctor's van is upside-down.'

She follows this by making a clay face. In the mouth she puts a yellow peg. The words I have written beside it are:

'That's my cat's nose. That's my cat's tongue.' [*Then in a separate space:*]
'It's you Miss.'

The visit the following day begins with her making another clay object. She copies another child's idea. He is making a shoe. She then uses his words to describe it. I have the words for this but no photograph. She said: 'It's a wee foo foo tail.'

Moving on from there to the big tray, she put the red shed flat on its back near the centre. On what was now the floor of the shed she placed ten little pink pigs and a black-and-white cow. They were all lying close together on their sides.

A reindeer was standing at each of the front corners of the dwelling and there was a yellow truck between them. Leaning against the truck was one of the 'Do Not Touch' notices. In the sand in front of this whole feature was a flat, pink, plywood pig. A piece of wooden fence was lying like a stray object in the lower right-hand corner of the tray.

She ended the visit by making another two clay objects. One was a square block of clay with a projection which looked like a small penis. She called it 'Tweetie Pie'. The other was also a block of clay with several smaller projections. She said this was 'a wee mouse shoe'.

Now it's the day before she made the mandala. All that has been recorded is a photograph of another clay object. It is a small block of clay with legs. She calls this one 'Cheeky'.

The following day she made a big tray in which the sand was flattened down. It had several enclosures. They contained the little pigs, upturned alligators, a soldier, a camel and a black-and-white cow. One enclosure had a gap in it which was blocked by a white stone and the container section of a haulage truck. Astride one of the fences which bordered another enclosure was a giraffe. There was a big reindeer in the top and bottom left-hand corners of the tray and at the right-hand side of it stood the flat pink pig.

The story began with these words:

'These are hills and these are roads.
I'm going to do that thing about the piggies again.
They're in the garden playing.'

It continued:

'The pigs are dying. The monkeys are trying to help them. They're trying to see if they can get them but they can't help them and the stone's rolling down the hill to see if they can die even further.
They're trying to bite arms and his legs and that's all.
Nothing else. Aye.

The piggies – they are still fighting till they get them – till they get them – till they get to them. And if they get to them they'll laugh and laugh and laugh until they're dead.

When they still laugh they'll be laughing.'

The final words were not about a tray as such; they were spoken about a drawing which was done with paint on grey sugar-paper and to which was added some of the tray materials.

In this 'picture' a small centre circle about four inches in diameter is enclosed by a square with sides of approximately seven inches. This itself was enclosed by a large rough circle of about thirteen inches in diameter. The space between the square and the outside circle was divided by lines into nine segments. Scraps of various sizes of Alcan foil were placed in each of the segments. A larger piece covered most of the centre area. On this was placed a bed and a small green-plastic play-pen. In each of these was a small Playmobile figure.

It was only as I looked at the photograph, several months after it had been produced, that I recalled reading something about mandalas and the Navaho Indians in a book by Jung. It was in fact *Man and his Symbols*, which he had been compiling at the time of his death and which was completed by Dr Marie-Louise von Franz. It says:

> For instance, the Navaho Indians try, by means of mandala-structured sand paintings, to bring a sick person back into harmony with himself and with the cosmos – and thereby to restore his health. (Jung, 1964, p. 213)

And over the page there was a photograph of a Navaho Indian sitting inside a painting. The caption reads: 'a Navaho makes a sand painting (a mandala) in a healing ritual; the patient sits in the painting' (Ibid., p. 214)

But there was more to this story, though it may well appear to be rather far-fetched. On several occasions around the time the picture was produced I had heard Ruth making sounds which were very reminiscent of the chants of the Haida Indians, on whose reservation I had worked when I lived on the Islands. I had passed on this observation to friends who understandably received it with some scepticism. Perhaps for those more familiar with Jung's ideas it would seem less obscure.

Then, only a few days ago, while looking for a definition of a mandala to assist me with a reappraisal of what she had made, I found the following words in Estelle Weinrib's *Images of the Self*. It could be that I had read them before but what I saw on this occasion came as a complete surprise and delight. On the evolution of sand play, under a sub-heading 'Magic Circles and Fantasies', she writes:

> The earliest precursors of sandplay therapy practitioners might be said to be those most primitive tribes who first drew protective magic circles in the earth.
>
> The nearest cultural parallel to sandplay therapy seems to be the sand painting of the Navajo religion wherein ritual sand pictures are used extensively in ceremonies of healing, as well as for divination, exorcism and other purposes.
>
> Pictures are made by chanters or medicine men and initiated assistants who mold and paint symbolic figures of sand on the ground, in prescribed arrangements, enclosed by 'guardian' boundaries marked in the sand. The figures represent mythic deities in human or animal form plus natural or geometric symbols, all of which are usually arranged in quadrants around a center, strongly suggesting a *mandala* form, except that the outer boundary (circular, square or rectangular) has an opening to allow evil to get out and good to get in. (Weinrib, 1983, p. 3)

These words completed a circle for me, bringing me neatly back to those Indian children in the Haida nursery school to whom this work owes so much.

On completing her mandala, Ruth said:

> 'You can have it, its yours.
> You can smash it if you want it.'

Then:

> 'It's bedtime for children.
> Bedtime for goodness.
> Bedtime for really really time and bedtime for goodness.
> And that's it.'

10 years 11 months   The boy of the brand new bridge.

Plate 1
**'HE'S GREETING BECAUSE HIS WEE BABY KING KONG
GOT TOOK AWAY.'**

8 years 10 months   The boy of the unsatisfactory breast.

Plate 2 '**THIS WEE BOTTLE IS FEEDING THE ROCK.**'

9 years 8 months   By the same boy as plate 2.

Plate 3 **THE STUCK HIPPOPOTAMUS.**

10 years 2 months   Master Eeps

Plate 4
'TRYING TO GET UP TO NEW YORK.'

12 years 10 months   David

Plate 5
**'THE BABY SURRENDERING
TO HAVE ITS NAPPY CHANGED.'**

Part V

Crossing the Great Divide

25

GUIDANCE FROM A STRANGER

There came a time in this whole endeavour when I felt I was standing looking across that great divide which separates educational practice from the domain of child psychotherapy and that perhaps I had acquired a bridge to the other side. Thinking over how I had arrived at this particular place, I had little difficulty in seeing the miraculous leaflet as the map for a journey.

The actual moment of knowing came as a delayed reaction to some remarks from a stranger, a man who had read the account of the earliest part of the journey, and who had ideas about where I might be going next. Most significantly, he spoke of the work being, and I quote, 'important in the context of the continuing neglect of children's emotional needs in educational settings'.

This was exactly what I needed to hear. The statement locked in very neatly with the proposals I had been developing for the application of the work. It helped rid me of remaining uncertainties about their validity, and supplied the impetus I needed to put the bridge in place and prepare to cross over it – even if I then made a hurried return.

These proposals had been taking shape from the moment I had started using the sand-tray materials. I had referred to them for a long time as a 'three-plank plan'. For someone in need of a bridge, and who had been engrossed in a project in which reconstructing the landscape was a significant theme, this title seemed especially apt.

Before moving on to introduce the proposals, I want to retrace my steps, to pick up on some of the issues which will require a closer look if the thinking behind them is to be fully appreciated. This will also allow me to say a bit more about the general climate in which the work took place.

My initial attempts to interest colleagues and administrators in the Child Guidance Service in the ideas I had developed on the course had been met with a mixture of scepticism and mirth. I had noted a pronounced tendency amongst many professionals not to take sand trays seriously. And, as can be imagined, even for those who held them in some regard there were marked disagreements, reflecting differing psychological orientations, as to how they should best be used.[34]

On a more down-to-earth level, in my excursions into the realms of psychotherapeutic talks and case-study presentations, I had detected a certain snobbishness about sand trays and am open to the accusation that my avoidance of the Lowenfeld approach may well have had a flavour of this. Even amongst the staff on the course, the ideas of both Lowenfeld and Klein had had a mostly negative influence on perceptions of therapeutic practice.

On several occasions, then and later, I witnessed the mere mention of Melanie Klein's name bring on an acute attack of scoffing. She appeared to be known solely as a purveyor of outrageous sexual interpretations of children's use of small toys. And, for one quite influential administrator in the Child Guidance Service, Margaret Lowenfeld was primarily associated with studies of the cultural differences of women immigrants – crossing the Atlantic Ocean to America in a liner – as revealed in sand-tray constructions.

But such antipathies were to prove mild in comparison to the hostility which I discovered could be provoked by speaking about psychoanalysis. Whatever the source of this – and I have insufficient knowledge of the subject to make reasoned comment – its relevance here is as a factor in the incident I am about to describe, for it had been declared by the main protagonist to be decidedly 'bad'.

---

[34] Worth mentioning in this respect, both as an illustration of such differences and for the information it provides on Margaret Lowenfeld's work, is the paper she read before the Medical Section of the British Psychological Society in 1938. Theoretical differences between Melanie Klein and Anna Freud are legend. Those between Klein and Lowenfeld were also quite lively, as the discussion which followed this presentation illustrates. This reference demanded inclusion, but I have chosen not to expand on it as it would take me too far away from the main story.

26

A Traumatic Mishap

There are unwelcome incidents on most journeys and this one was no exception.

In the introduction to Part Two I made reference to an incident which affected the outcome of the work. In keeping with the proposition that the constructive expression of unpleasurable events can contribute towards their resolution, there has been a strong temptation to write it up in detail but, as any attempt to be objective would probably be impossible, I intend to focus mainly on some of the ways in which it advanced my understanding of the children's difficulties.

As the environment became more established, there was a slow build-up of the kind of antipathies which had been around as the work with David began. A gathering-in of negative feelings and projections eventually culminated in my receiving a verbal mugging from a male colleague. I was unprepared for the extent to which I had been affected by this incident. It was only several years later, when preparing a paper on the alleviation of the effects of trauma in young children, that I fully acknowledged to myself that it had been traumatic for me and that its effects would, in several respects, be similar to those experienced by the children.

Looking back it seems surprising that it took me so long to make the connection, but it has to be remembered that I knew nothing about the subject when I set out. That the room evolved into a place where children felt able to address concerns associated with trauma was both an inadvertent side-product and a major outcome of the work.

But to the benefits.

Whilst I would obviously have preferred a less painful route to the understanding gained, nothing I experienced led me to doubt that I was on the right track with the environment. Based on my own difficulties, it certainly confirmed my view that the prospects of finding someone capable of lining-in exactly with another's psychic tribulations are so limited, it was at least a good starting point to create a kind of smorgasbord of a resource; one which could be utilised in a manner and to a degree commensurate with an individual's idiosyncratic requirements.

I also became aware that the degree of damage caused by such incidents is likely to be a reflection of a constellation of factors. In my own case the main ingredients were the condition of the receiver, my psychological suitability as a receptacle for what was projected, the violence of the attack – coming as I believe it did, from a breaking-through of split-off and severely repressed hostilities which 'belonged' elsewhere – and the shock factor.

Of these it was the condition of the recipient of the stimulus which interested me most, as I came to believe that what the children and I had most in common was a weak base. To spare the reader some head-grinding self-analysis, I will be extremely brief and declare that mine at that time was mainly the consequence of ingrained neurotic tendencies aggravated by drastically depleted resources, due to an overload of work both inside and outside the unit. On some days I was working with as many as fourteen children, while my evenings were spent studying and writing up the work. I had also chosen to take on a few referrals after school hours, from educational psychologists working within the service. I did this in part in a mistaken effort to demonstrate the value of the work. My duties as an assistant head teacher also took their toll.

As for the children, I believe all those who had shown the most bizarre and out-of-control behaviour, which was subsequently and inevitably found to be associated with traumatic incidents, were the ones who throughout their early lives had had insufficient structure and nourishment to enable them to make any steady developmental progress. And their prospects for achieving any future psychological stability were also being continually jeopardised by further unremitting exposure to unpleasurable experiences within chaotic home circumstances. These were the children who would be struggling and yet were expected by some to make constructive use of the opportunities for social, psychological and intellectual development which were available to them in school.

It seemed obvious from such observations that everything possible should be done to counteract the negative input and compensate for any lack of nourishment, in conditions which would contribute towards a strengthening of the base – and that this should be happening as early as possible in their life at school.

27

Looking for an Analyst

It will be apparent by now that the method of working which was eventually devised had come about through a mixture of influences and adversities, of which the work with the children was just one. Of the more personal of these, the incident just described was undoubtedly the biggest adversity. An experience which equalled it in influence, but thankfully not in negative impact, was the search for an analyst – and then trying to settle with one.

Over a period of about five years I tried several therapists. This provoked the charge, from a psychiatrist amongst others, that my unwillingness to settle with any of them implied more about my pathological difficulties than their inadequacies. I accept this charge, in part. I could counter, however, with the view that I was unable to settle because I never found what I was looking for. Cost was undoubtedly a factor. I may well have stayed with one of the more expensive practitioners much longer, had I been much richer.

In appraising these encounters, I placed alongside them those of friends involved in a similar pursuit. I acquired further information from published accounts of therapeutic relationships and was able to form some clear ideas about what kind of therapy I personally would have liked and, following on from that, what I should be trying to provide for the children. The amalgamated effect of these experiences and observations was a relatively thin body of knowledge, but one with a strong enough frame on which to hang my ideas about distorted symbol formation and the possibility of bringing about radical change in how the children were functioning.

I was impressed by my inability to bring about any substantial change in my own functioning and by how prolonged and troublesome an undertaking it can be – for both the therapist and the client. I was left with one clear image. It had been evoked spontaneously and its sharpness has remained undiminished.

It is of a mound of stones, a bit like a cairn that one finds on a mountain. Some of the stones around the edges have been loosened up in the process of the therapeutic work and can be moved around and repositioned, but the central edifice remains virtually unaltered. It turned me time and time again towards the view that what goes wrong for most of us begins at such an early age, and can be so difficult to resolve when allowed to consolidate, that all efforts should be made to prevent it happening in the first place.

And having reached this position, there was again only one place to go. As far as the application of the work was concerned, any comprehensive moves towards achieving this would have to be made at as early an age as possible, within the children's own school.

The stranger's remarks, the traumatic mishap and the pursuit of the analyst were to play a major role in shaping the proposals and placing them firmly in a preventative mode.

In common cause with the previously stated aims of counteracting the negative and compensating for any lack of nourishment in conditions conducive to a strengthening of the base, the children would also require an on-site opportunity to give ongoing constructive expression to their concerns. This would be necessary not only as a means of bringing about their resolution but also to pre-empt their consolidation into the more intractable difficulties which become less amenable to remedy at a later stage of their development.

How these ideas might be implemented in practice is what the three-plank plan was all about.

28

THE THREE PLANKS

Each of the planks took shape at different times during the course of the work. Each has its individual strengths and could be employed alone, but only the central plank would be strong enough to carry anyone over to the other side of the divide. Together I believe they would make a wider bridge and guarantee a much safer crossing.

As much of what I have had to say so far has been in the form of a story, I have opted to continue in the same mode and will present the planks in order of their chronological appearance.

ONE: A PRIMARY RESOURCE

From the earliest times of using the sand-tray materials, my appreciation of them had left me increasingly perplexed as to why, when they had been known and used by art, play and child psychotherapists for more than seventy years, they had not been made more available to more children. By the time I had left the unit I had introduced sand trays to over 150 children. Of these, only one child had not been immediately enthusiastic about the prospect of using them. This was a boy who had taken a brief look before retreating swiftly to the other side of the room, where he pressed his back against the wall as if to make certain he would not be inadvertently drawn back towards them. Only lack of time and authority, and certainly not of interest, prevented me from making enquiries about the possible causes of this behaviour.

The idea that it might be possible to use sand trays as a resource material in a classroom in a mainstream primary school had occurred to me when I first observed how attractive they were to the children. But it received a substantial boost during a two-week period of teaching practice in a school for children with moderate learning difficulties. This was another requirement of the course on Special Needs. The thoughts I had then about how they might be employed in a mainstream setting have remained virtually unchanged.

There had been no special planning for their introduction into my room during that practice: I merely placed a sand tray and a selection of toys and objects on a table in the vicinity of all the other materials which are usually available at choosing time. There were only ten children in that particular group, and I realise that this is a much smaller number than is found in the average primary class, nevertheless, the materials were remarkably easy to manage. The organisation of trays with a class of over twenty-five obviously would be a much livelier proposition and I am not underestimating the challenge. Given adequate supplies, however, I see no reason why the materials could not become as manageable as a good supply of Lego.

To facilitate their effective management, the basic furniture requirements would be two storage cabinets on wheels. These are advertised in the catalogues of the major suppliers of school equipment. Described as 'ten drawer storage units' they are approximately 670 mm x 360 mm x 740 mm. They are open at the front and come complete with small plastic drawers. In one cabinet would be drawers containing sand. Their size and weight would be such that the children could transport them with relative ease to their desks. The second cabinet would house a collection of small toys, objects and other materials. The child would make a preliminary selection into a small box or other container suitable for carrying it over to their sand tray. These cabinets could be moved between classrooms if necessary.

In keeping with all that has been said so far, I anticipate that the use the children would make of the materials would be roughly commensurate with the three levels of symbolic activity which were previously identified. For those children who were relatively at ease with themselves, their use would be predominantly pleasurable. It would involve the creative exploration of thoughts and ideas and the processing of relatively recent information and experience. Some measure of success in resolving concerns of a relatively slight nature would be expected.

At the other end of the scale would be the children who were demonstrating through their constructions that they were in need of a lot more help than could be provided in the classroom. Many of these would be children who had already let this be known through other means such as their work and general behaviour. In this group also would be the quieter children who were attempting to deal with their concerns by illness or withdrawal.

And between these two groups would be the third and probably largest one, encompassing the children who were capable of going in either direction and who, if the initiatives I am suggesting here were effective, would begin to make definite moves towards the lighter use of the materials.

As regards the role of the teacher: given the sand-tray's capacity for the short-term absorption of intolerable issues, there could be distinct advantages for both the child and the teacher in allowing the sand trays to be used at various times throughout the day. The decision to do this would obviously be dependent on the teacher's inclination and experience. As a material which can be used in a very structured way, I believe that most teachers would find it a lot easier to manage than informal play.

For those teachers who became genuinely interested in dealing with the more contentious issues that a child might wish to bring to them, my own view is that any opening-up in class should not be encouraged. Children need to have a clear expectation of what is available to them, and what is given to one has to be available to all. On a practical level alone it would not be feasible. I think a better option for any teacher who is strongly drawn towards tending to the child's emotional concerns would be to learn how to manage an environment themselves. The qualities considered desirable for anyone interested in doing this will be discussed below.

In my initial enthusiasm for using sand trays as a resource material, I had imagined them functioning in isolation from any other provision, not out of any kind of preference but more as a consequence of blinkered thinking. I did not welcome them at the time, but obstacles which had hindered my progress in setting up a pilot study in a primary school in the early years proved to be blessings. They gave me time to realise it would be unfair to children who were carrying around serious unresolved issues not to have in place a readily available back-up facility in which to address them. I had taken it for granted that the established psychiatric, psychological and social work agencies would be drawn upon to provide what was required. A slow and steady awakening to the difficulties which were likely to arise, in respect of both the timing and quality of that assistance, brought into sharper focus the option of establishing an environment in every school. And if that is considered too idealistic and costly to contemplate, then one environment for a group of primary schools within a local area.

Such a policy should conform well to the needs of the many teachers who prefer a strictly formal classroom role and who would appreciate having the opportunity to arrange for a child to take their emotional concerns elsewhere and return later, ready to settle to the educational tasks in hand.

Two: A Creative Environment

By the end of my fourteen years in the unit I had undoubtedly found a way of working which was well suited to my temperament and to many of my specific strengths and weaknesses. Given the opportunity to work with children between the ages of five and eleven, who had been severely damaged through a combination of abuse and deprivation, I would probably have accepted the challenge. Whether I should have been allowed to do so is another question. Including the work I had done outside the unit, I would also have been reasonably confident of helping younger children sort out some of the more temporary short-term entanglements which so easily occur for them.

My experience during the first seven years, some of it with children whose concerns were of an extremely serious nature, was acquired in a manner not dissimilar to that employed by a non-swimmer who is thrown into a pool and manages to keep afloat. I certainly was not proceeding with the work on the grounds of any formal assessment of my fitness for the task.

Likewise, for many of the most troubled children, their referral and placement in the unit was rarely the outcome of some well-defined policy. They were most likely to be children whose difficulties had been inadequately assessed previously, and who were now acting-out in such a way as to be in need of some kind of special provision. Others were accepted because a more appropriate place did not exist or was too costly or was unavailable at the time it was needed. Most of the big boys, whose predicament had been such a motivation to change my ways, belonged in one or other of these categories.

We were all really just thrown in together; those who did not manage to stay afloat usually moved on. My own survival, which had been in question on several occasions before the mugging, was certainly much more to do with good luck than careful management. And I was not alone in receiving this kind of initiation. At that time the majority of teachers who took up positions in child guidance units had no experience or training in taking care of children who are severely emotionally disturbed.

There can be benefits, of course, from having been thrown in at the deep end, and after thrashing about I surfaced to find I had acquired certain useful characteristics. These were of limited value in pre-sand-tray days, when most of my energy was spent tending to symptoms rather than causes but, after their discovery, they were to take on an added significance. They have a relevance to the proposals, as will be explained shortly.

Whereas the management of the environment within the unit was always to some degree in a state of unsatisfactory flux, the procedures employed inside it, as suggested before, achieved a stability verging on the routine. The challenges posed by the child's concerns remained undiminished but, with the vehicles capable of moving them closer to resolution running smoothly, questions began to stir about the environment's suitability for use by other workers in other settings. Thoughts of a tentative kind gained solidity during the process of writing up the work and finally fell into place, as an essential part of the bridge, shortly after the stranger had spoken.

To begin with, apart from the children's enthusiasm for the materials, I was enthralled with the level of dynamic creative activity which, on numerous occasions, was being generated in the room. Leaving aside the question of whether or not this kind of activity could produce the therapeutic effects to which I was aspiring, it was a marked improvement on the wearing-down days of old. It fired in me the kind of evangelical fervour I had not experienced since the discovery of religion during early adolescence.

At first I merely wanted to tell other workers how interesting it was. Later on, as my prospects for continuing the work in the unit were diminishing fast, I began to contemplate its transferability in relation to a specific colleague. Here was someone else who had learned to stay afloat through the deep-end treatment and who had been naturally supportive of the environment throughout its development. I acknowledged her earlier as the co-progenitor of the ideas on double or parallel nourishment. She was the first of many workers from various disciplines with whom I talked over the years, on a formal and an informal basis, about the feasibility of using the approach in other settings. There was never any lack of interest or enthusiasm from those on the ground. It was only with those who aspired to walk above it that I met with any resistance.

During that whole period I consulted workers who were employed in hospitals and special schools, in residential and children's homes and in social work offices. Many of them expressed serious frustration at being unable to work more constructively with the children in their care. This was in part a consequence of having neither sufficient time nor adequate premises, but there was always the issue of what kind of approach they should employ. There was a widespread feeling at this time that the systems which were in place to assist children were as ineffective for them as they were unsatisfactory for the workers. Only those professionals who were unable to acknowledge the paucity of their own contribution would have disputed this. A culture seemed to have developed in which the needs of the child were disappearing further over the horizon as the foreground got more crowded with more managers. Constantly active in the pursuit of new and self-aggrandising schemes, and bent on providing evidence of their organisational virility, they appeared to be more interested in finding ways of moving the children around the system than the means for keeping them in one place long enough to effectively address their difficulties.

After several years of registering such observations, I eventually extracted from them a point of view which suited my purposes. There was a need among many workers for a more structured approach to the children in their care and there was a need among many children for a more structured response to their concerns. And it was between these two sets of needs that I began to think the environment had a place.

There was nothing new in what the environment had to offer. Nothing was done which had not been done before. Most of the principles and procedures being employed came directly from those which have been tried and tested for decades and were common to most art, play and child psychotherapy rooms. Any differences between this method of working and other established therapeutic approaches was in the particular mix of materials and procedures which were employed and in the emphasis given to each.

The features which gave it its own particular quality were those which had served me well in overcoming some of the disadvantages of having had no formal training in child psychotherapy. And it was these same features which I thought should facilitate its adoption by others. In no special order, they were the way in which the children's symbolic productions were allowed to proceed mostly unhindered and, partly as a consequence of this, the emphasis which was placed on the procedure of Talk and Draw. And there was the extent to which I leaned on the materials and procedures; a posture which had been adopted partly as a consequence of trying to keep my unanalysed self out of the picture.

To reaffirm my position on the children's symbolic output, particularly as it manifested itself in their sand-tray constructions: choosing not to respond to it directly is not seen as a licence to ignore it. Whilst an in-depth understanding of the symbolic is not a requisite of this way of working, it can inform so much else of what the children bring to the room that every effort should be made to acquire one.

Circumventing the symbolic, however, does put the emphasis very firmly onto the procedure of Talk and Draw as the medium around which the worker makes direct contact with the child. It is through the support it provides to the child, during their efforts to put words to deeds often never before spoken of, that it plays a dynamic and pivotal role in the resolution of their concerns. And it is in the timing of this interaction, and the sensitivity with which the words are received, that this feature of the approach becomes the one to make most demands on the worker.

Yet as a medium for dealing with the relatively mundane practical matters in the child's everyday life, Talk and Draw can not be bettered. For a worker starting out, this is a technique around which a steady and satisfactory expertise can be achieved. Having the paper and the pen gives it a grounding which makes it so much easier to manage than the more nebulous exchanges which, in my experience, are implicit in a novice's attempts to deal in symbolic interpretations.

I had several reasons – or perhaps I should say excuses – for wanting to keep myself out of the picture as much as possible. Fear was undoubtedly one of them. One of the lessons I had learned about myself from the various therapists I had met was not to trust what I might be bringing to any interaction with another human being, either child or adult. I wanted to be as sure as possible that my own unresolved concerns would not get mixed up with those of the children.

A further incentive came from listening to the stories told by therapists at case-study presentations. I had been alarmed by some of the descriptions given, even by apparently experienced practitioners, of the roles they acted out with children during therapeutic sessions, while they gave a sort of interpretive running commentary on the proceedings. I wanted to avoid getting into similar situations if this were at all possible. I knew I would have been decidedly inept at sustaining an objective distance from the processes taking place.

It is difficult to be clear at this stage of the work whether I began to lean more heavily on the materials as a means of playing safe and distancing myself from the kind of interactions described above, or whether the extent to which I was already leaning on them had facilitated the distancing ethos. Whichever way it came about, I believe that it was my life-long affection for creative activities, and all that goes with them, which was again seeing me through this latest challenge. Just as they had eased my burden of inexperience in the Haida nursery school and then during the first seven years in the unit, they were providing an alternative route to the stability of setting essential to any therapeutic endeavour.

It may well have been a poor substitute for the kind of security of setting advocated by Hanna Segal but if I had waited to get straightened out to the extent indicated in the two concluding sentences, I would have never got started. It is one of several statements I read when I was well into the work and which had a profound cautionary effect. She writes:

> It is often through a failure of arranging a sufficiently stable management that the analytic treatment comes to grief. The analytic setting must provide for the patient the kind of holding environment in which his relationship to the analyst can develop without being broken up by the patient's psychosis. This necessitates, obviously, such things as reliability and regularity of the hours, a certain uniformity of the setting, a feeling of physical safety if the patient is violent, etc. But the analyst himself is a very important part of the setting. He must remain constant and not vary his role so that the patient's phantasies of omnipotent powers over objects can gradually undergo a reality testing. With secure management of the background and proper analytic setting, the analysis can proceed. (Segal, [1981] 1986, p. 133)

I would like to make my position quite clear on this. I had sensed from the the start that I should only be proceeding with a well-analysed self, and to help calm my feelings of rightful trepidation I had tried to reassure myself in two ways. To begin with I adopted the same approach as I had to increasing my understanding of the symbolic, that is, I decided it should be perpetually sought but not allowed to keep me from getting on with the job. And so it was as regards my understanding of self. I would do all I could to improve it, both inside and outside analysis, aiming at least for a clear recognition of all the worst bits, even if I were unable to root them out.

And I did something more immediate and concrete, although less honest. I comforted myself with the view that the environment provided nothing much more than a focused opportunity for constructive creative expression. There may well be circumstances in which it could be restricted to that use alone, but I think the more probable scenario would be one in which the children's need to get help with unresolved issues would precipitate an offloading which neither child nor worker would want or be able to stem.

When the local play therapist first heard about what was happening in the environment, she observed that it was functioning like one of those skips which are placed empty in a street one day and have been filled to overflowing overnight with unwanted rubbish from almost every house in the neighbourhood – much of it having been hoarded for years awaiting just such an opportunity. And so it would be for children in the neighbourhood of an environment.

By now it should be apparent that the feature which more than any other convinced me that this approach could be utilised by others was the extent to which it leaned on the materials and procedures. However, in order for them to carry any worker through the more robust challenges implicit in this kind of work, and do it as effectively as I am suggesting it can be done, their integrity would need to be rigorously protected. Using the analogy of a boat: this one was built through a long process of trial and error and it had survived some stormy waters before its main specifications were decided on. Now it may well be that many of these could be changed substantially and the boat would continue to stay afloat. As I have no way of knowing this, I think it is only reasonable, at this stage, to propose that anyone wishing to sail similar waters should learn how to handle this particular model before making any major alterations.

The selection and the quality of the materials, the care with which they are arranged and displayed, and the refinements of the procedures, as they were developed in the environment, are all interwoven into the fabric of this approach. Its strength depends on adhering closely to them. If the materials in the room are allowed to get lost, misplaced and damaged, children arriving at the door will not see before them a place fitted out with care for their purposes but just another of those disordered settings which are common in so many areas of their lives. I am aware that putting pressure on children to treat the environment and everything in it with care might be considered unacceptable in some therapeutic approaches, creating constraints which could only aggravate some of their difficulties. This may be so, but, in leading the children towards the constructive expression of their concerns and as a means of assisting them to take control and responsibility for them, it worked well for me. And in the role for the environment which I am about to advocate, I believe these limits would not only be necessary but would be essential to its effectiveness. Of course, as the experience of the worker grows, these parameters can be softened to fit the circumstances.

There is one other important factor to emphasise. For a room like this to function well it needs a worker who is as willing to sweep, wash, wipe and keep the materials in order as he/she is to improve his/her expertise in meeting the more esoteric challenges. Indeed, having a worker who is a good cleaner may well be the characteristic which sets this approach apart from others.

If the features described above give this plank its strength to carry the worker, then there are certain qualities which would be required of any worker who desired to walk it. I am returning here to the characteristics which I had acquired, in some measure, by the end of my seven-year survival course in the unit, and which I will now suggest would be required by anyone who wanted to manage an environment. I have identified them as a back wall and a capacity to nourish; and the more one has of each, the better would be one's prospects of being able to help the children.

As a rough guide only, the ideal nourisher with a back wall would be someone who could convey, on first meeting, a sense of having the strength and capacity to receive and survive whatever a child might bring to them, and who has been given enough nourishment in their own lives to be genuinely inclined towards giving out rather than taking in. They would be strong on caring, capable of setting firm and consistently fair parameters and would manage their relationships with children with warmth, compassion, common sense and ingenuity.

I accept that identifying workers with the two basic characteristics might be more difficult than I, in my enthusiasm for this work, imagine, but I am buoyed by the reactions of several fellow workers who, on being asked to consider this matter, were at least confident of recognising people who had a back wall. They were less certain about identifying those who can nourish. Having become more aware of the false selves and the repressed hostilities which can lurk in otherwise quite kind and genuine-looking people, seeking them out is not a task I would relish myself. This is a difficult issue, and although I see no easy way round it, I would anticipate being able to locate wise counsel on how to best to proceed with it.

Just as the children using the sand trays in the classroom would fall into three main groups, I anticipate that those who found their way to the environment would divide roughly into the children who were able to settle and make constructive use of what was on offer, and those who could not. This is a simplistic division but adequate to lead in to the next deliberations.

For those who were able to settle, the environment would function in the various ways indicated throughout this account. To recap: at one end of the scale would be the entirely pleasurable and predominantly aesthetic exploration of thoughts and ideas, a kind of creativity for its own sake, and at the other end would be the mainly unpleasurable struggle involved in trying to come to terms with intractable deeds and dreads. Again, it is mainly towards the range of concerns between these two extremes that the proposals are being directed.

As I discovered in my own work in the unit, all the children who came to the room, however profound their deprivation and however cumulative the effects of their intolerable experiences, were also carrying around relatively minor unresolved issues. The majority of these were associated with traumatic incidents and events of various types and intensities, and were amenable to some remediation with a subsequent reduction in distress and an increased capacity to be at ease with themselves and others.

Again, this will only ever be validated if put to the test in practice but, in my assessment, many of these difficulties could be dealt with effectively by a worker who had the makings of a nourisher with a back wall, several years of work experience with children with emotional and behavioural problems, and a period of three to six months of learning how to manage an environment through practice.

No matter how successful the work might prove to be in the long term, in gradually reducing the number of children whose problems were being seriously aggravated by neglect, there would inevitably be a backlog of those who had been left too long and who would be demanding more than the worker could give and more than could be provided within the school setting.

Taking it for granted that the staff and everyone else concerned with the children's welfare would be doing their best to sustain them in their local school, the number who were on the edge of being settled would obviously be largely dependent on the abilities of the worker. But some line would have to be drawn as regards how far the worker should be expected to go in persevering with a child.

I would suggest that with a child who continued to push hard against what was on offer, and who was unable to make any constructive use of the environment after being given access to it for at least an hour each day, five days a week, for about a month, then for both the good of the child and the worker it would probably be necessary to call a halt. Whether the child's failure to make use of

the facility was a reflection of the seriousness of the child's difficulties, or the limitations of the worker, the same criteria would still
hold good.

For these are the children who should never have been allowed
to get to this stage in the first place and whom the proposals are
intended to help in future. And they are most likely the ones who
are being so overwhelmed by what is happening to them in their
out-of-school lives that no matter how much was being provided in
school, it would be insufficient to counteract the negative input.
And these are also the children who will behave in much the same
way when they are referred to special day-provision.

The serious reservations I now have as regards this kind of
provision may yet be too coloured by my own negative experiences
in one of them. It is undeniable, however, that if the preventative
measures I am advocating were to be vigorously implemented, and
carried through with some degree of success, the need for such
provision would be on a diminishing road to redundancy. Unless
such day facilities have a formal therapeutic component capable of
addressing the underlying causes of the children's difficulties, rather
than just modifying their behaviour (an achievable short-term aim
in a small protective setting), or some change for the better can be
effected in the rest of their lives, it is extremely doubtful that the
gains necessary to sustain them in the long term can be
brought about.

This raises the question of my work with David. As the account
of the early days with him shows, it was touch and go whether either
of us would come through the experience. Looking back, I realise
that I took him on without properly querying my right or ability to
do so. I would be less arrogant now and, if placed in a similar
situation, would agree to do the work only if I had the unequivocal
support of the staff and the parents, and those administratively
responsible for the child's welfare. And then perhaps only if it were
to take place in a residential setting.

Going back to those on the edge of being sustained in school: until
it becomes possible through psychological tests and assessment to
identify the children who have insufficient internal strengths to
withstand the negative input in their lives, and who are at risk of
never being able to consolidate enough of the positive to tolerate it
in future, then the line that can be drawn between letting go and
hanging on will continue to be blurred – to the detriment of far too
many children.

There are of course numerous reasons for the procrastinations and neglect from which many children suffer. It is certainly not through malice that they are not helped soon enough. Many of them do become the victim of a new teacher or social worker who, based on nothing more than a mixture of misguided and ill-informed optimism, makes a false assessment of the possibilities for change in the child or in the home circumstances, and is convinced that where others have failed, they can succeed. And yet paradoxically often it is only through the stubborn determination of a worker that a child becomes convinced that there is a genuine possibility of success and is motivated to get onto a more positive road.

A further major cause of delay is the understandable reluctance to give a child time out when they are very young, but I have never known a big boy in the unit who had not been identified as having serious problems from the age of three or four. And if ever parents and workers somewhere along the line do find themselves in agreement that some kind of respite would benefit the child and the parents, then it is the dearth of appropriate residential provision which gets in the way. This difficulty could be eased greatly if a more imaginative and flexible approach were taken. If one were to wipe the slate clean and rethink what was required, based on the needs of the children and the parents, there is no doubt that something other than what is presently on offer would be devised.

Whereas I believe that these proposals are capable of bringing about a substantial shift in the balance of provision for children with emotional and behavioural difficulties, the already obvious need for a wide range of quality residential care would still remain.

Just as the environment would be the back-up for the sand trays, so an environment would require to negotiate its place alongside the various medical, psychological and psychiatric services and agencies responsible for the welfare of children. What that place might be would be best settled through practice.

I am well aware that a complex network of issues has been raised by the observations made above, and that they deserve a longer look than the sidelong glances they have been given in passing. Not least of these is the child's relationship with its family. Whilst my main focus of interest has been on the child's capacity to create a coherent sense of self, whatever the adversities, I have taken it as given that, alongside the initiatives I am proposing, all options would be explored and all efforts would be made to bring parents and children into as close and co-operative a contact as possible.

As my destination has become clearer I must admit to being eager to cover the final stretch as quickly as possible, but there are a number of applications of the work which have been sidelined by concentrating on the use of the environment in a primary school setting and I would like to bring some of these back into view before moving on to consider the third plank.

On hearing about children who have been badly affected by the troubles in Northern Ireland, the air disaster over Lockerbie, and the wars in Kuwait and Bosnia, I felt convinced that the environment's capacity to help absorb the acute effects of recent trauma would make it an effective resource for the children who had been involved as victims or observers in such situations. I am also convinced that the same capacities would make it equally effective in a hospital setting with children attending on an in-patient or out-patient basis, who are experiencing pain and distress associated with the causes and effects of accidents, and the treatment of acute and chronic illness.

One of the environment's advantages over individual counselling, in common with other similar approaches, is that it can accommodate small groups of children, with each child able to draw from the resources available as their needs dictate. And, as Talk and Draw is only utilised at the child's instigation, there is no pressure of any kind to use words. The benefit of having an early opportunity to externalise an unpleasurable stimulus is not only that it brings about some immediate relief, but that it can also discourage the child from attempting to deal with it internally, through the more debilitating strategies of illness and withdrawal. These were first introduced in 'Three Reluctances' in relation to the boy who got overheated. A study was suggested, in which the effects of regular opportunities for constructive externalising could be monitored in children with symptoms for which no physiological or organic cause had been identified. At the time, I envisaged this being set up within a hospital. Recent information on the increased incidence of asthma and a reduction in the general levels of health amongst primary age children in some parts of the city in which I am writing this, persuade me that such a study might be incorporated into an evaluation of these proposals, if they were to be implemented in a primary school.

The ideas for using the environment within a primary school setting came initially from a concern for the children I knew in the unit, many of whom came from the most deprived areas of the city.

I can see no reason, however, why it could not be just as effective with children who are much better provided for materially but who are just as likely to get into similar emotional entanglements. In my opinion it would fit as comfortably into a formal academic establishment as it would into the more rugged places for which it was first considered.

THREE: A COMPLEMENTARY NOURISHER

This is the third and smallest plank, but in terms of its preventative capacity it could be the strongest.

The ideas on the benefits of feeding, both real and symbolic, were expanded on in the chapter on Symbolic Reconstruction and this plank came about as a direct consequence of these. It concerns the role of school as a complementary nourisher. The proposition here is that the behaviour of the majority of children who came to the unit reflected drastic early feeding experiences, aggravated by traumatic incidents and events, and that their prospects of being sustained in mainstream education would be markedly enhanced if their local primary school made some attempt to complement the nourishment they were receiving at home. If children were getting very little then this lack could be substantially compensated for, and if they were getting plenty, then a top-up would be an added bonus.

Based on the work in the unit, a simple initiative suggested itself. It was to use food to produce the maximum benefits for the children by arranging to have it given out and shared in a very structured manner – verging on the ritualistic – as an integral part of the day's routines. It would require to be done in conditions conducive to a positive internalising of it, that is, with the generosity and care which should accompany all interactions between workers and children.

To be more specific, I would advocate giving a drink and a biscuit on arrival each morning and at morning break, a proper formal lunch, and a sweet on leaving at the end of the afternoon; one which would pass the teeth quickly. Ideally it would involve every class throughout the school but, if it had to be restricted because of cost or other considerations, at the very least it should be made available to those in their first two years. Sanctions of all kinds which might be in use in the school, as a means of trying to modify unacceptable behaviour, would rarely if ever include the withholding of these.

If the ideas on strengthening the base, which were floated earlier, are too hard to digest, this plan can be considered solely as a means of improving the children's everyday experience of school and their perception of it.

If one imagines a child coming from a home situation in which neither consistent care nor regular feeding is provided, and where those on whom they depend are persistently preoccupied with their own emotional and financial struggles, then waking each day to the prospect of a few hours of relative peace and comfort, whatever else might be available, could make a significant impact on their lives.

Again I am in no way advocating a withdrawal of parental and family responsibility for children. Nor am I suggesting that school should be viewed as a place which takes over these responsibilities. I am merely suggesting that if the basic ingredients for a child's development are not available to them at home, then society surely has a duty to attempt some compensatory provision. And the best place for this has to be school. No one anywhere disputes that a well-fed and secure child is more likely to make effective use of the social and intellectual opportunities which are on offer in a good educational establishment. Any reservations regarding the children who may have developed a difficult relationship to food should not be allowed to overshadow the benefits which might accrue to the others. But it would require an awareness of the issue on the part of the adults in charge and a willingness to seek professional guidance if necessary.

In the face of the desperate conditions in which many children try to make their way, I accept that these suggestions could only make a slight contribution to loosening the hold which deprivation has on their lives. I also accept that any real change will only come about through social policies geared to improved opportunities for employment and the provision of adequate housing. I think, however, that the squeeze on deprivation needs to come from all directions, and it would be a privilege to have given it even a good hard nip.[35]

---

[35] After all that has been said and done; if I had to limit myself to one suggestion to improve the welfare of children in general, I would reintroduce milk into all nursery and primary schools; making certain, of course, that it was given out with as much care as possible.

29

IN A FIELD OF POSSIBILITIES

The stranger whose words I quoted at the beginning of this section recommended that if I were ever to write a full account of the work, I might explain why I had, to use his words, 'picked this particular theoretical orientation from the range of psychodynamic approaches available'. These remarks were made in response to a reading of 'Externalising the Unpleasurable' in its original format, and I doubt if he would have bothered to make them had he read about the surrounding events; for I think it would have been apparent that I had neither the knowledge nor the inclination to make such a choice.

As my encounter with Margaret Lowenfeld gives some indication, I had wanted to avoid getting stuck on any one particular road early in the work, lest I would have difficulty getting off it later. If I had ever been in doubt about the human propensity for getting stuck, all uncertainties had fled when faced with the frequent manifestations of the condition in the children's sand-tray constructions; especially those of the boy of the unsatisfactory breast.

Still, the remarks do raise the question of what choices I made and whether they could have been radically different. For example, I have wondered whether reading biographies of Freud could have exerted such an influence that I was irretrievably drawn towards adopting a psychoanalytic perspective on the work. Or was mine a kind of psychoanalytic personality type whose life experiences would allow no other leaning? And even, on a cellular level, were the neurons in my brain assembled[36] in such a way as to make some of the basic tenets of psychodynamic theory unavoidable objects of desire?

And yet I have continually refuted the suggestion that what the children and I did in the room was predominantly psychodynamic in nature, and have felt quite justified in doing so. I have no objections to having ended up in that particular field if that is where

---

[36] Neuronal assemblies were encountered initially in the work of Jean-Pierre Changeux (1985). They were promising a neurobiological explanation of persistently distorted symbolic features and signalling (through the associated ideas of Hebb [1949] and Kandel [1975]), the future direction of the work.

I genuinely belong but, accepting that the discrepancy between perception and reality can be vast and I could be misleading myself about this, my intention throughout has been to keep my ideas as loose and unaligned as possible. I was again strongly influenced in adopting this position by Lawrence Kubie who writes in the paper 'Psychoanalysis and Scientific Method', from which I quoted earlier, 'If one can set up a situation in which one eliminates all of the factors that distort free association, one is polling the human thinking machine' (Kubie, 1959, p. 71),

I reasoned that if some of this kind of thinking was getting registered in the records and being communicated to me without too many distortions, then what I had found out would have a resonance with ideas from a diversity of disciplines. It would then only require someone with an overall knowledge of theories of the mind to help me identify which fields I had crossed en route. And there might even be the possibility of having contributed to a better understanding of how children function – which was after all what I had hoped to accomplish when I set out.

On a more practical level I feel less inclined to leave the field so open and there is one proposition I would like to see firmly planted and taking root there.

It is that the request to be good, which is frequently used to powerful effect in the furtherance of children's personal and social development, needs an equally weighty counterbalance if it is not also to prove detrimental to their emotional and physical health. And, in accordance with all that has been written here, this can be achieved through the provision of opportunities and conditions which are fully supportive of their need to let it be known how bad they might feel.

Whereas the proposals which have been presented, along with other measures of a similar kind, can be helpful in advancing such objectives within a variety of settings, they are capable of making only limited inroads into what is essentially a much wider and more general need. For this to be met, more of a cultural shift will be required; one which stems from an increased understanding of the damage which can be caused to children when, fearing the loss of affection and security, they feel pressured to conceal their concerns. This work began with a focus on a particular group of children within a specific setting, but by its close it was this issue, with implications for all children, which had laid claim to the title of the book and been accepted as the distillate of the entire experience.

REFERENCES

Axline, V. (1964) *Dibs: In Search of Self.* Harmondsworth: Penguin, 1971.

Beres, D. (1965) 'Symbol and Object', *Bulletin of the Menninger Clinic* 29 (1): 3–23.

Bettelheim, B. (1972) 'Regression as Progress', in P. L. Giovacchini, ed., *Tactics and Techniques in Psychoanalytic Therapy.* New York: Science House, pp. 189–99.

Bion, W. R. (1962) *Learning from Experience.* London: Maresfield, 1988.

Bowyer, L. R. (1970) *The Lowenfeld World Technique: Studies in Personality.* Oxford: Pergamon.

Cassirer, E. (1944) *An Essay on Man.* New Haven, CT: Yale University Press.

Changeux, J-P. (1985) *Neuronal Man: The biology of the mind.* Oxford: Oxford University Press, 1986.

Eickhoff, L. F. W. (1952) 'Dreams in Sand', *Journal of Mental Science* 98: 235–43.

Erikson, E. H. (1972) 'Play and Actuality', in M. Piers, ed., *Play and Development: a symposium.* New York: Norton, pp. 127–67.

Fairbairn, W. R. D. (1943) 'The Repression and the Return of Bad Objects (with special reference to the "War Neuroses")' in *Psychoanalytic Studies of the Personality.* London: Routledge & Kegan Paul, 1952, pp. 59–81.

Freud, S. (1900–1) *Interpretation of Dreams,* in James Strachey, ed. *Standard Edition of the Complete Psychological Works of Sigmund Freud,* 24 vols. London: Hogarth, 1953–73, vols 4 and 5.

—— (1901) *The Psychopathology of Everyday Life. S.E.* 6, 1960.

—— (1920) 'Beyond the Pleasure Principle', *S.E.* 18, 1955, pp. 7–64.

—— (1926[1925]) 'Inhibitions, Symptoms and Anxiety', *S.E.* 20, 1959, pp. 87–175.

—— (1933 [1932]) 'Anxiety and Instinctual Life', *S.E.* 22, 1964, pp. 81–111.

—— (1940[1938]) 'An Outline of Psycho-Analysis', *S.E.* 23, 1964, pp. 144–207.

Furst, S. S. (1967) 'Psychic Trauma: A Survey', in S. S. Furst, ed., *Psychic Trauma.* New York: Basic, pp. 3–50.

Guntrip, H. (1952) *Schizoid Phenomena, Object-Relations and the Self.* London: Hogarth, 1968.

Harding, M. E. (1961) 'What Makes The Symbol Effective As A Healing Agent', in G. Adler, ed., *Current Trends in Analytic Psychology.* London: Tavistock.

Haynes, H., White, B. L. and Held, R. (1965) 'Visual Accommodation in Human Infants', *Science* 148: 528–30.

Hebb, D. O. (1949) *The Organization of Behaviour: A Neuropsychological Theory.* New York and London: John Wiley.

Hood-Williams, J. (1974) 'Child Psychotherapy at the Institute of Child Psychology', *Journal of Child Psychotherapy* 3(4): 73–83.

Jones, E. (1916) 'The theory of symbolism', in *Papers on Psycho-Analysis.* London: Balliere, Tindall and Cox, 1920, pp. 129–86.

Jung, C. G. (1964) *Man and his Symbols.* London: Aldus.

Kalff, D. M. (1980) *Sandplay.* Santa Monica, CA: Sigo.

Kandel, E. R. (1975) 'Psychotherapy and the Single Synapse', *New England Journal of Medicine* 301(19): 1028–37.

Klein, M. (1957) 'Envy and Gratitude', in *Envy and Gratitude and Other Works.* London: Hogarth, 1984, pp. 176–235.

Krebs, H. A. and Shelley, J. H. (1975) *The creative process in science and medicine. Proceedings of the C. H. Boehringer Sohn Symposium.* New York: American Elsevier.

Kris, E. (1956) 'The Recovery of Childhood Memories in Psychoanalysis', *Psychoanal. Study Child* 11: 54–88.

Kubie, L. S. (1953) 'The Central Representation of the Symbolic Process in Psychosomatic Disorders', *Psychosomatic Medicine* 15(1): 1–7.

—— (1957) 'The Psychodynamic Position on Etiology,' in H.D. Kruse, ed., *Integrating the Approaches to Mental Disease.* New York: Hoeber-Harper, pp. 14–33.

—— (1959) 'Psychoanalysis and Scientific Method' in S. Hook, ed., *Psychoanalysis, Scientific Method, and Philosophy: a symposium.* New York: New York University Press, pp. 57–77.

—— (1966) 'A Reconsideration of Thinking, The Dream Process, and "The Dream"', *Psychoanal. Q.* 35: 191–8.

—— (1974) 'Impairment of the Freedom to Change with the Acquisition of the Symbolic Process', *Psychoanal. Study Child* 29: 257–62.

Langer, S. K. (1942) *Philosophy in a New Key.* Cambridge, MA: Harvard University Press, 1957.

Lippman, H. S. (1956) *Treatment of the Child in Emotional Conflict.* New York: McGraw-Hill.

Lowenfeld, M. (1939) 'The World Pictures of Children: A Method of Recording and Studying Them', *B. J. Med. Psychol.* 18: 65–101.

Mahler, M. S. (1969) *On Human Symbiosis and the Vicissitudes of Individuation* vol. 1. London: Hogarth.

Miller, P. R. (1969) *Sense and Symbol: A textbook of human behavioural science.* London: Staple.

Milner, M. (1955) 'The Role of Illusion in Symbol Formation', in M. Klein, Heiman, P. and Money-Kyrle, R.E. eds, *New Directions in Psycho-Analysis.* London: Maresfield, 1977, pp. 82–108.

Money-Kyrle, R.E. (1955) 'An Inconclusive Contribution To The Theory of the Death Instinct', in M. Klein, Heiman, P. and Money-Kyrle, R.E. eds, *New Directions in Psycho-Analysis.* London: Maresfield, 1977, pp. 499–509.

Moody, R. (1956) 'Symposium on Jung's Contribution to Analytical Thought and Practice', *B. J. Med. Psychol.* 29: 9–14.

Novick, J. and Hurry, A. (1969) 'Projection and Externalisation', *Journal of Child Psychotherapy* 2 (3): 5–20.

Piaget, J. (1951) *Play, Dreams and Imitation in Childhood.* London: Routledge & Kegan Paul.

—— (1970) 'Piaget's Theory', in P. Mussen, ed., *Carmichael's Manual of Child Psychology* vol. 1, 3rd edn. New York: John Wiley, pp. 703–32.

Pickford, R. (1975) 'Expression of Thoughts by Means of the Lowenfeld Sand Tray "World" Material', in I. Jakab, ed., *Transcultural Aspects of Psychiatric Art, Psychiatry and Art,* vol. 4. New York: Karger, Basel, pp. 188–92.

Read, H. (1943) *Education Through Art.* London: Faber.

Rodrigué, E. (1956) 'Notes on Symbolism', *International Journal of Psycho-Analysis* 27: 147–58.

Roffwarg, H. P. Muzio, J. N. and Dement, W.C. (1966) 'Ontogenetic Development of the Human Sleep-Dream Cycle', *Science* 152: 604–19.

Rycroft, C. (1972) *A Critical Dictionary of Psychoanalysis.* Harmondsworth: Penguin.

Segal, H. (1986) 'A Psychoanalytic Approach to the Treatment of Psychosis', in *The Work of Hanna Segal.* London: Free Association Books and Maresfield, pp. 131–6.

Schopenhauer, A. (1883) *The World as Will and Idea* vol. 2. Trans. R. B. Haldane and J. Kemp. London: Trubner, 1886.

Schur, M. (1958) 'The Ego And The Id In Anxiety', *Psychoanal. Study Child* 13: 190–220.

Singer, J. L. (1973) *The Child's World of Make Believe.* New York and London: Academic.

—— (1975) *Daydreaming and Fantasy.* London: Allen and Unwin.

Sylvester, E. and Kunst, M. (1943) 'Psychodynamic Aspects of the Reading Problem', *American Journal of Orthopsychiatry* 13(1).

Tustin, F. (1981) *Autistic States in Children.* London: Routledge & Kegan Paul.

van Baal, J. (1971) 'The study of symbols: the works of Freud, Jung and Cassirer; symbolic anthropology', in *Symbols for Communication: an introduction to the anthropological study of religion.* Assen: Van Gorcum, 1985, pp. 137–69.

Weinrib, E. L. (1983) *Images of the Self.* Boston, MA: Sigo.

Werner, H. and Kaplan, B. (1963) *Symbol Formation: An Organismic-Developmental Approach to Language and the Expression of Thought.* New York: John Wiley.

Winnicott, D. W. (1945) 'Primitive Emotional Development', in *Through Paediatrics to Psycho-Analysis.* London: Hogarth, 1982, pp. 145–56.

—— (1966) 'The Location of Cultural Experience', *International Journal of Psycho-Analysis* 48: 368–72.

—— (1971) *Therapeutic Consultations in Child Psychiatry.* London: Hogarth.

—— (1977) *The Piggle: An Account of the Psychoanalytic Treatment of a Little Girl.* Harmondsworth: Penguin,1980.

INDEX

strain, 45
therapy for effects of, 210
tray stories
children's comments as
completed, 20–1, 49
'drawn', 136–7
photographing, 7, 29–30, 58,
153
and reading difficulties,
167–70
recording of comments, 58
tray stories, samples
Bedtime for Goodness, 175–88
The Brand New Bridge, 154–7
David's, 148–53
Escape from a Water Box,
157–9
Getting Run Over at the Bus
Stop, 160–1
King Kong Gets Buried, 153–4
A Professor who was Mad on
Sports Cars, 167–70
Sausage, Egg and Beans, Four
Times, 164–7
Sooking and Sooking like a
Mad Man, 161–4
Trying to Get Up to New
York, 170–5
trust, lack of, 125–6
Tustin, Frances, *Autistic States in
Children*, 83–4

unpleasurable, expression of
the, 45–6, 61

van Baal, J., *Symbols for
Communication*, 51
von Hug-Hellmuth, Hermine, 7

Weinrib, Estelle, 75
Images of the Self, 188
on protected space, 60
Werner, Heinz and Bernard
Kaplan, on symbol
formation, 76
Winnicott, D.W., 58
'squiggle game', 59
'The Location of Cultural
Experience', 60–1, 63
The Piggle, 4
*Therapeutic Consultations in
Child Psychiatry*, 59
worker
need to subdue personality,
26
qualities required, 205–8
role of, 58–9, 199, 203–4
World Material (Lowenfeld's),
5, 7, 18
worries, 'getting out', 33–4,
136, 175

Index by Auriol Griffith-Jones